Quality Service, Competitive Business: setting the standard in customer service

Howard Kendall

First published in the UK in 2010

by
BSI
389 Chiswick High Road
London W4 4AL

© British Standards Institution 2010

All rights reserved. Except as permitted under the *Copyright, Designs and Patents Act 1988*, no part of this publication may be reproduced, stored in a retrieval system or transmitted in any form or by any means – electronic, photocopying, recording or otherwise – without prior permission in writing from the publisher.

Whilst every care has been taken in developing and compiling this publication, BSI accepts no liability for any loss or damage caused, arising directly or indirectly in connection with reliance on its contents except to the extent that such liability may not be excluded in law.

BSI has made every reasonable effort to locate, contact and acknowledge copyright owners of material included in this book. Anyone who believes that they have a claim of copyright in any of the content of this book should contact BSI at the above address.

BSI has no responsibility for the persistence or accuracy of URLs for external or third-party internet websites referred to in this book, and does not guarantee that any content on such websites is, or will remain, accurate or appropriate.

The right of Howard Kendall to be identified as the author of this Work has been asserted by him in accordance with sections 77 and 78 of the *Copyright, Designs and Patents Act 1988*.

Typeset in Garamond Pro and Franklin Gothic by Monolith, www.monolith.uk.com
Printed in Great Britain by Berforts Group, www.berforts.co.uk

British Library Cataloguing in Publication Data
A catalogue record for this book is available from the British Library

ISBN 978-0-580-68515-6

Contents

Preface	vii
Foreword	ix
Acknowledgements	xi
Introduction	xiii
1. Understanding your customers	1
2. Great customer service and experience	12
3. Customer service strategy, culture and objectives	32
4. Customer service people	53
5. Customer service processes	76
6. Customer service technology	100
7. Measurement of customer service success	120
Conclusion	148
Bibliography	150
Appendix A: Figures	157

Preface

This book is all about good customer service. Whether you want to expand your customer base, boost customer loyalty, increase your public profile or increase your profit margins, this book will tell you, in simple terms, how to achieve it.

The BSI (British Standards Institution) has long been developing standards that relate to service or services in many forms. This book is an excellent way of drawing attention to those standards and how they are relevant and important today.

I have been involved in customer services for over 20 years and have been passionately involved in setting standards and advancing best practice in this area. I have been leading BSI's customer service standards group for over eight years and have been responsible for the UK input on BS ISO 10002:2004 *Quality management – Customer satisfaction – Guidelines for complaints handling in organizations* as well as leading the group that developed the BS 8477:2007 standard for customer service. This means that I am in a unique position to write this book.

In researching the book, I sought out some of the best and most practical examples that you will be able to adapt for your own use and, added to the excellent backdrop of standards and advice from experts, the book represents a true reflection of contemporary best practice in customer service.

I wish you every success in achieving your customer service goals.

Howard Kendall

Foreword

When I first started in service quality over 20 years ago, it was an uphill challenge to convince colleagues that customer service was a tough, serious business concept. It was even more challenging to convince them that it should permeate the whole organization and not just the front line. Sometimes they did not even recognize that they had customers at all!

Not any more. That bit of the task is behind us. The more enlightened among us agree that service quality lies at the heart of competitive business. And the reason, more or less, is repeat business. We want our customers to keep coming back. Better still, we want customers to tell their friends what great people we are to do business with. The entire rationale for providing a better service than our competitors is to *sell more to existing customers and to attract new ones*.

In the public sector, it is no less important. Here, we need to ensure value-add for our customers – they want us to give them value for their money. Improved customer service leads to higher reputation, lower costs and greater trust.

We have all bought into the fact that it makes sound business sense to deliver good service – but that, nowadays, good is not good enough (because satisfied customers still leave us). What we need to do is to go that bit further and *delight* our customers. We need to give them a *topbox service* experience that is far beyond that of our competitors or peers – that is what leads to real loyalty.

So, the question on people's lips is no longer *Why deliver world-class service?* but *How can we deliver world-class service?*

At the Institute of Customer Service, we were repeatedly asked over the years how our research helped us to answer that question. We were asked to come up with some kind of model that would help people to understand what their organization needed to do to deliver great service. So, we developed the *Institute of Customer Service Model for World-Class Customer Service* and I am delighted to see that it is referenced in this book.

I was very happy to write the foreword to this book because it gives lots of practical examples of how to do best what matters most to our customers.

But the most important lesson in the customer service journey is about taking personal responsibility. A motto of mine is that I would rather have to apologize later than to ask permission in advance. How often have we heard people saying – *don't tell me, tell them up there?* Lack of support is often used as an excuse for doing nothing. So, I will leave you to ponder this:

It is better to light one candle than to curse the darkness. Confucius

Robert Crawford, Director, Client Services, ICS

Acknowledgements

Firstly, I am really grateful to my wife of 32 years, Ruth, who has had to put up with my waking up in the middle of the night and jotting down ideas for the book on my notepad, in addition to the early morning wake-ups, which is when I work best.

Secondly, thank you to the great teams I work with at the Service Desk Institute (SDI) and The Consultation Institute (TCI), that have both contributed ideas and suggestions and given me the confidence to take time out to write this book.

A further thank you must go to all the contributors in the industry who put up with my continual pressure to share their expertise and advice. This was essential to a book that needed to reflect the current best practice across the industry, and particular thanks should go to Cathy Lilley and Robert Crawford at the Institute of Customer Service, who provided some excellent input from Institute of Customer Service sources.

Sam Cranston has worked tirelessly as my researcher on the book and has been a magnificent trawler of the internet and written sources. He contributed magnificently to the diligence of the referencing process.

Lastly a huge vote of thanks to Fiona Tucker, my commissioning editor at BSI, who has been a constant source of guidance on the particular requirements of publishing such a definitive book on this subject. I could not have written this book without her advice and encouragement.

Introduction

Setting a goal

It is essential to set ourselves goals, something to aim towards. In this book, my goal is simple; your goal is perhaps not as simple. My goal is:

- to write a straightforward, easy-to-read book that confirms all that you *should* know about customer service and challenges you to think about what you need to learn and actions you need to take to make it better for you and your customers.

Because I cannot assume what your goals are, I have left a blank space for you to insert your own. You are unique, and that is a point we often forget about customers. Although there are obvious assumptions that I can make about what you *might* set as a goal for your reading, they are not going to cover everyone: I have as much chance of working out your goals as scoring for England in the World Cup Final!

However, you may wish to consider these as possibilities:

- to learn about all aspects of contemporary customer service and what it involves;
- to check that you are not missing anything in your current service strategy or plan;
- to improve current customer service practice;
- to develop new ideas and freshen up your service plans and ethos;
- to identify key skill or behaviour improvements for your people.

Your goal is:

A recent survey by the People 1st Sector Skills Council (SSC) found that '63% of employers in the sample felt their staff's customer service skills were not sufficient to meet their business needs' (2009). Given that the SSC serves the hospitality industry, covering hotels, restaurants and entertainment facilities, whose businesses are dependent on service, this is a big concern.

World Class Customer Service... for 2012 and Beyond – Summary Report (2009)

Background information

In its most simple and effective form, good customer service is the customer's complete satisfaction with the product or service that they have just bought and received. This will include all sizes of organizations that develop products or provide services – from a sole trader to a large company – and encompasses customers ranging from someone buying fruit from a market stall to someone buying a fleet of aircraft to start a new airline. Although the *scale* of the service may differ significantly in the B2C (business-to-consumer) market and the B2B (business-to-business) market, the key elements of good service remain the same.

Although the principles of customer service can be very simple and grounded in common sense, they can also provoke controversy and debate. Those working in customer service can have a vested interest in making it more complex than it is. I should know: I make my living from telling people how to 'do' customer service better.

It makes life frustrating when management speak exhorts staff to 'delight the customer', develop the 'customer value proposition' and discuss their 'net promoter score', while not really grasping that you need to understand the basics of service and help your staff to provide them to deliver really outstanding service. Without that basic knowledge, all of the jargon is simply that – jargon that will deliver little or no value.

Any service point is a vital interface between an organization's customers and its operational delivery units. This applies whether the customers are external – receiving goods or services supplied on a truly commercial basis – or whether they are internal – receiving goods and services in order for them to do their jobs productively, which in turn allows them to serve external customers better. It does not matter what the goods or services are.

This book gives readers a definitive what, who, why and 'how to' guide to the current best ways for setting up and maintaining a good customer service strategy and staff. It identifies what a truly great customer experience is and how to deliver it. By bringing together the current best advice and guidance, and by using the standards developed by the BSI, the book will provide a true 'best of the best' benchmark for customer service today.

BS 8477:2007 *Code of practice for customer service* helps to set in place mechanisms to ensure levels of customer service that meet the needs and reasonable expectations of customers and helps organizations to be competitive in the marketplace. The standard stresses the importance of increasing levels of customers' positive emotional experience with an organization's services and, through this, building and maintaining customer loyalty and customer retention. The standard helps organizations to increase their service efficiency and to lower complaint rates and also seeks to aid compliance with fair trading and consumer protection laws, which is essential to avoid damaging brand reputation.

Customer service operations and methodologies are well established in many organizations; in others there are none. This book will help you to align your customer service strategy with the goals of the business within which it operates and to deliver a high-value and memorable experience consistently to your customers that keeps them coming back to you.

The book highlights the structure, processes and organization of the people and resources you need – whether it is a small organization or a large multinational corporation – and offers advice on how to achieve the best operational mix. It will also cover how to work with third parties, as often the service you deliver will contain elements that are delivered by others. This is especially true with internet-based businesses, which have initiated an explosion in logistics companies to service online shopping and subsequent fulfilment activity.

Technology now has a key role in every business, and the book identifies the key types of technology and their role in service.

There will be a heavy emphasis on how to lead, direct and motivate your staff, with considerable focus on how best to achieve a great customer experience. Service is above all about people delivering to people, even if the method of delivery involves no direct people contact at all, such as with internet-based purchases.

It can be difficult to determine what is really important to the customer and how to relate that to an organization's aims. We will look at what targets you should set and measure and what are the right performance statistics to track successful service delivery and improvement, including how to track and handle complaints.

There are 'real life' examples and exercises to put the theory into practice, and in each chapter there are lessons or action points for you to consider.

A simple web portal, www.customerservice.co.uk, has been developed alongside the book. Its aims are to share news and views on the latest developments in customer services and to connect you to other sources of advice and guidance.

Although many organizations will already have mature customer service practices and will be reaping the benefits of them, there are many that will not. Both will gain from the good advice available here.

There is one more thing to bear in mind: you and your organization's customer service operation can make a big difference to the quality of people's lives – either positively or negatively. This book sets out to make sure yours will be considered a positive one!

1

Understanding your customers

The basics

It is an accepted fact that you cannot deliver great service to customers unless you understand them – at least to a degree. It is surprising then that many organizations and small traders make little effort to do so, especially as it can make a significant difference to their sales, profitability and customer retention.

BS EN ISO 9004:2000 *Quality management systems – Guidelines for performance improvements*, states that the success of the organization depends on understanding and satisfying the current and future needs and expectations of present and potential customers and end-users, as well as understanding and considering those of other interested parties. Furthermore, there are several research reports that underpin the direction provided by the standard. The Institute of Customer Service research report *Customer Priorities* gives this simple 'top 10' list of priorities:

- overall quality of the product or service supplied;
- friendliness of staff;
- handling problems and complaints;
- speed of service;
- helpfulness of staff;
- handling enquiries;
- being treated as a valued customer;
- competence of staff;
- ease of doing business;
- being kept informed.

(Institute of Customer Service, 2006)

The order in which those priorities apply will change with each customer, and with each customer the order will change depending on the circumstances. It is up to the customer service provider – you – to understand the following key statement for every one of your customers:

What does this customer, whom I'm dealing with right now, want?

Anticipating customer needs

To identify some key issues to focus on with your customers – and hence build your understanding of them – I have chosen a 'day in the life of a typical customer' for analysis.

> ### Case study 1
>
> Jane walked from the car to the station entrance and noticed that she had just a couple of minutes before her train was due to leave. She wondered if she had time to get her usual cappuccino and newspaper from the single kiosk, which had a couple of people queuing.
>
> She decided to try, as she really fancied that coffee – and as luck would have it one person walked off as she joined the queue. Julie, the server at the kiosk, was dealing efficiently with the one man in front of her, and Jane was sure she'd make the train. The man in front wanted to pay by card and Julie explained she didn't take them, and he then started searching his pockets belatedly for the change to pay for his coffee.
>
> Just as Jane thought she'd have to leave it, the man found the coins and paid. Jane smiled at Julie and said she'd like her usual cappuccino and paper. Julie smiled back and passed her a lidded cup and paper, saying 'I saw you coming across the car park and didn't want you to miss out on your coffee so I doubled up on the last order'. She waved her off to the platform, just 30 seconds before Jane's train departed.

The coffee and newspaper kiosk attendant had anticipated Jane's needs based on previous experience, and she exceeded Jane's expectation this time. As a small local independent business, it had clearly done the simple things right. A diligent and observant member of staff who had taken the time to understand what was important to Jane in the very short 'moment of truth'[1] has guaranteed that Jane is more likely to stop and spend at the kiosk than to walk past. As the owner of this business, the only real way to improve on the service would be to add additional product lines to grow the customer spend at each visit.

---

[1] A 'moment of truth' is any point of connection to or interaction with customers, where they could be impressed (or not) by the service experience given. See Jan Carlzon's book, *Moments of Truth*.

Going back to the BS EN ISO 9004 guidance, customer understanding is both for now and the future. In Chapter 2, we will address at length the issue of what constitutes great customer service. We will also evaluate the more recent trend of 'the customer experience'. This trend has spawned a whole industry built around the concept of ensuring that your organization delivers a great 'customer experience' to your customer to gain their longer-term loyalty to you.

At this stage it is important to understand the concept only as it applies to understanding your customer. Amit Kakkad (under the direction of Chris Voss, Emeritus Professor of Operations and Technology Management at the London Business School) states in his 2006 research report *Wanted: Chief Experience Officer* that 'customer experience is increasingly being seen as a real and sustainable differentiator between competing organizations' (Figure 1) and that 'the use of customer experiences to create value has been called the experience economy' (Kakkad and Voss, 2006).

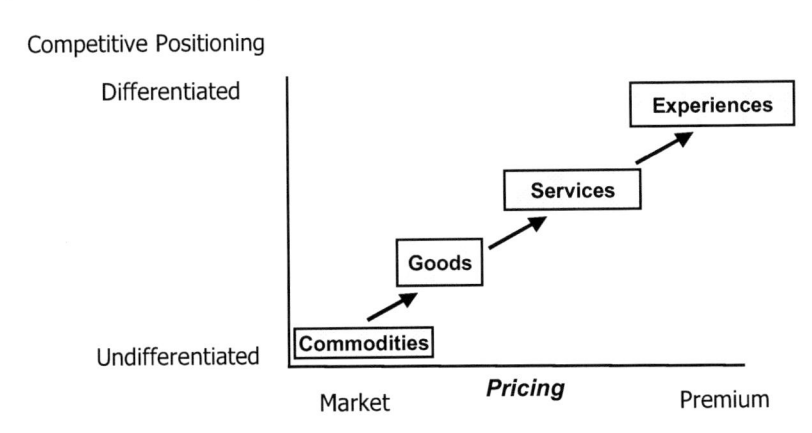

Competitive Positioning

Source: Pine and Gilmore

Figure 1. Experiences create value (Kakkad and Voss, 2006).

A Nokia Siemens 2009 research report *How to Generate Customer Loyalty in Mobile Markets*, based on a survey of 12,000 people in both emerging and mature markets, found that most customers in mature markets are open to better offers or more attractive packages from the competition, which means that no service provider can be complacent and expect their customer base to stay with them over time, unless they take specific steps to please their customers (Nokia Siemens Network, 2009). The following chart – one of many in the report – breaks down the understanding of what customers find to be their 'moments of truth' with their service provider. This allowed Nokia Siemens to focus effort precisely on what their customers valued.

The report also found that dissatisfaction also drove decisions. Many 'churners' (those who leave for the competition) move because of a bad experience. Globally, almost 38 per cent of churners say that they switched because of dissatisfaction, and a comparable 39 per cent of non-churners say that dissatisfaction would make them consider churning. Establishing an understanding of the customer and what they want is a prerequisite. The Nokia Siemens report showed that customers leave both for better offers and because of general dissatisfaction. *This* is a fundamental illustration of the financial impact of poor service, and the benefit of great service (Nokia Siemens Network, 2009).

Avis, for example, who rents cars worldwide, found that training to understand the different cultures and attitudes of customers throughout the world was essential to improve their customer service and to reduce the number of complaints. Staff in Europe participated in a multimedia delivery training system to accommodate the different learning styles of the Avis agent incorporating:

- Video scenes of culturally different coffee shop scenarios which were then played above Avis counters.
- Words to read, highlighting the differences shown in the video scenes with examples to use.
- Listen and learn to hear the examples shown.

The academic information on the differences in cultural upbringing needed to be relevant to the whole customer journey in the organization, as well as clear to the staff on how and when to apply different behaviour to different customers, which might sometimes be uncomfortable and alien to the customer service provider's natural behaviour. Hints and tips were supplied to the staff to establish what they should do, what they should say, and when and why they should say it (Court, 2009).

The results for Avis were quick and obvious. The complaints dropped considerably because customers were being served differently to suit not only their personality profile but also their cultural idiosyncrasies. This allowed the customer-facing staff to react differently and more relevantly to the individual customer and therefore prevent any festering complaint being reported once the customer left their office (Court, 2009). Very often large organizations make the mistake of assuming that, for example, renting a car in the UK is the same as renting a car in Italy, or buying a hamburger in the USA is the same as buying a hamburger in South Africa. That is a mistake that is not made so often nowadays.

Customer retention drivers – impact in %

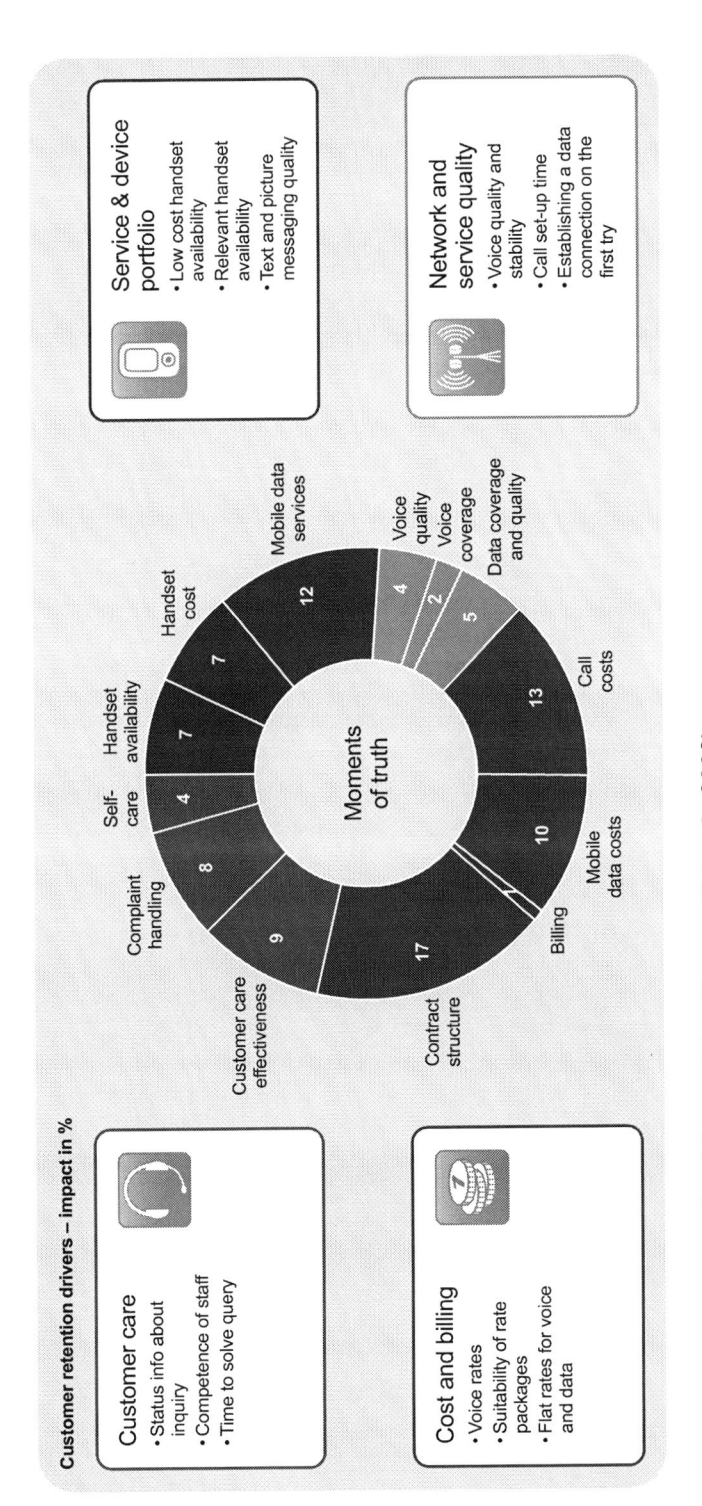

Customer care
- Status info about inquiry
- Competence of staff
- Time to solve query

Cost and billing
- Voice rates
- Suitability of rate packages
- Flat rates for voice and data

Service & device portfolio
- Low cost handset availability
- Relevant handset availability
- Text and picture messaging quality

Network and service quality
- Voice quality and stability
- Call set-up time
- Establishing a data connection on the first try

Moments of truth:
- Mobile data services: 12
- Handset cost: 7
- Handset availability: 7
- Self-care: 4
- Complaint handling: 8
- Customer care effectiveness: 9
- Contract structure: 17
- Billing: 10
- Mobile data costs: 10
- Call costs: 13
- Data coverage and quality: 5
- Voice coverage: 2
- Voice quality: 4

Figure 2. Customer retention drivers (Nokia Siemens Network, 2009).

Understanding an immediate customer need

So far we have looked at understanding and anticipating customers and their likely requirements from our organization, but how do we respond to an immediate need?

> **Case study 2**
>
> Jane's heel caught in the train door and broke. The station heel bar attendant told her that he could not fix it while she waited, but that they kept spare pairs of trainers for just such situations. He found a pair in Jane's size, and told her she could pick up her shoes that afternoon. She laced up the trainers and left her shoes at the heel bar for collection on her way home. She reasoned that at least she would still be at work in good time and had a story to tell her incoming clients!
>
> That afternoon, Jane picked up her shoes from the heel bar. The repair had restored her left shoe so the scuffing round the point that had stuck was almost invisible, and the heel was once again sturdily attached.
>
> The attendant pointed out that a tip sheet for care of this type of shoe had been included, along with a voucher for 20 per cent off if she brought in another pair of shoes for repair within three months. Although the bill was a little more than Jane would have paid back where she lived, she was delighted with the repair and service and mentally made a note to bring in the pair of shoes that had been lying in the bottom of her wardrobe that she had not bothered to fix after last summer.

The heel bar provided Jane with an immediate solution to an emergency need – and also provided follow-up care that probably has Jane hooked as a customer for life. This is one of the ultimate aims of customer service as indicated by Colin Shaw and John Ivens' book, *Building Great Customer Experiences*, in which they established seven philosophies for building great customer experiences. The very first of these is that great customer experience is a source of long-term competitive advantage (Shaw and Ivens, 2002).

This heel bar example is based on the real-life Timpson organization, founded by John Timpson and now run by his son James. They take great care to understand their customers through interaction with their staff, and the Timpson family are often seen visiting the shops in the chain to ensure that each shop delivers service to a similar standard. Although the provision of trainers was a value-added service that I invented for the purpose of the story, Timpson has already adopted the personal service approach that Jane experienced and also replaces watch straps, sells umbrellas and offers a dry cleaning service to sell more at their strategically placed heel bars.

Turning a one-off 'distress' purchase into a 'customer for life' means understanding not just what your customer wants, right now, but also understanding what might get them to come back, again and again. For this business, it is very much about impressing with the first visit, then offering the incentive discount voucher for a return visit. This policy could turn the customer from a £25 single buyer into a buyer who spends £25 every four months for the rest of their life.

A commonly used technique for understanding Jane, or any type of customer, is customer profiling. There are several types of profiling in use today. These four categories, sourced from www.morebusiness.com (2007), illustrate some of the types in use today:

- *affinity profiling*: studying buying habits to determine what kinds of product particular customers require;
- *demographic profiling*: looking at details such as geographical location, marital status or age, to determine what you might be able to sell to various types of customer;
- *psychological profiling*: by understanding a person's psychological motivations you should be able to understand their preferences. For example, you could assume that a woman seen in a supermarket car park driving a Mini Cooper and dressed in designer jeans might have an interest in making a fashion statement.
- *lifestyle coding*: this helps you to understand the way a person leads their life by looking at their hobbies and habits. Hence a person who is interested in American football may also have an interest in baseball or in collecting American sports memorabilia.

Understanding the business customer – B2B

Is the B2B (business-to-business) service environment different? It is often said that people change when they arrive at their workplace, which is reason enough to assume that B2B service might be different. There are other factors that might make it easier to sell to or service a customer, for example that in their business role they typically will be spending someone else's money. There are other factors that might make it more difficult, for example you might be dealing with a business in financial trouble and hence a limited budget, or perhaps you are dealing with a staff member under pressure to reach a particular price target. In the latter cases it will put pressure on your own margins and the cost of service will come into question.

However, whether you are in a B2B or B2C environment, the principles of customer service still apply.

> **Case study 3**
>
> Jane noticed the file she had asked for was waiting on her desk, but there was no sign of the exhibition stand graphics she had ordered from the design shop. The shop had promised that the designs would be delivered in time for her meeting, as they were a key part of the work Jane had prepared for the client campaign.
>
> Jane called the designer who had been responsible for her job only to hear that he had not been able to courier the designs across last night and that they were on their way this morning. It would be touch and go whether they made it by the end of the meeting, let alone in time for Jane to check them before the clients arrived.
>
> Knowing that she was frustrated with him, the designer offered to email the designs so that at least the clients could look at them on-screen. Left with little choice, a disgruntled Jane took this option. Two hours later – just after the clients had left – the stand designs arrived.

Jane has clearly experienced inadequate service from the design agency. It largely revolved around the poor timeliness of an otherwise good quality product. This is the key factor in delivering services to other businesses: you need to hit, or to exceed, their delivery expectations, with a good quality product. This is not in itself very different from B2C service, but often B2B sales require deeper levels of understanding of your customer.

The design company designs might have been excellent, but the failure to understand and meet a critical deadline and customer expectation will restrict their growth and could kill the business. Cutting-edge designers will win business, but tardy service and lack of attention to detail will lose it just as quickly.

Viking Direct, a supplier of office stationery and equipment, identified in the 1990s that supplies of stationery often took a week or longer from order to delivery. They understood from their customer research that customers often found this too long a lead time. As a result they introduced a simple catalogue and typically delivered orders within 24–48 hours. This practice changed the marketplace and is now the accepted standard.

In the Institute of Customer Service research paper *Excellence in Managing the Business-to-Business Customer Relationship* customers who felt that their suppliers were providing a good service in a B2B relationship were typified by the following: responsiveness, consistency, loyalty, trust, integrity and transparency (Institute of Customer Service, 2007).

Summary

Many of us will have been able to relate to Jane's stories of service in her 'typical day'. It is, however, still quite uncommon for us to consider the various aspects of a person's 'typical day' with a view to offering them better service – at least on a regular basis. Do you think that Jane has ever been asked about the services she receives during her day? The design company, a typical small business, knew little about Jane's time requirement.

The service world is changing, as shown by the Nokia Siemens and Avis examples, but it still tends to be mostly large businesses in mass consumer markets that undertake 'customer understanding' research. Success and failure in business today happens much more quickly than it ever has before – witness the recent demise of a number of large organizations, such as Lehman Brothers and Woolworths. The need to understand the business environment and customer requirements has never been greater, whatever the size of your business.

Jane's day was fairly ordinary and common to millions of people, but she experienced several 'touch points' that gave organizations the ability to affect her life in either a positive – or negative – way. This information is vital, and every organization should at least understand their basic customer 'moments of truth' so that effort can be focused on them.

It can be easy to ignore such an ordinary customer day and the opportunities and threats it presents to us. Often we focus on the sophisticated, high-end customer, or get bogged down with statistical and demographic analysis and CRM (customer relationship management) systems, when a simple assessment of the key parts of a customer's day and our role in it would reap huge benefits in delivering a great service experience and retaining a loyal customer.

> **Case study 4: Harley-Davidson**
>
> Owners of Harley-Davidson motorcycles who are members of the Harley Owners Group (HOG) clubs around the world are very visible advocates for the brand. Not only do they buy the motorcycles, but they also actively accessorize with Harley-Davidson equipment for their choppers, wear a vast array of Harley-Davidson clothing and enthusiastically participate in Harley-Davidson events. Starting with fewer than 50 members in 1983, HOG has grown to more than 800,000 members, more than half of whom attend at least one Harley-Davidson event per year. HOG members, as a consequence, know a great deal about what it means to be Harley-Davidson owners.

> How important are HOG zealots to the company? Harley-Davidson does almost no advertising, depending, instead, upon its community of advocates to purchase both motorcycles and logo gear and to spread the word to others. Customer advocacy has an impact on virtually every area of company activity. As John Russell, managing director of Harley-Davidson Europe, has said: 'If it is important to the customer; if it's a good insight; if it's a good point of understanding and connection to the customer, it makes its way into business processes and becomes part of what we do.' That is powerful recognition of the value of direct customer input.
>
> Michael Lowenstein (2005) at: http://www.customerthink.com/article/let_in_sunshine_customers_help_grow_business

Learning points

This chapter has focused on the start point of customer service: *understanding your customer's basic needs and desires from the product or service that you have to offer.*

The most important points to remember are:

- understand what you are selling and what the customer expects from it;
- understand and track your customers' key event dates where possible so that sales and service opportunities are not lost;
- understand how and where your customers buy from you as it will guide you on expectation and further opportunity;
- understand who your customers are, i.e. what type of people want your product or service;
- maintain and keep developing your understanding of your customers and keep developing and enhancing your products and services to mirror customer need and desire changes.

The following is a short list of techniques and examples to consider and learn from (both positive and negative).

Techniques

- Always ask yourself: What does this customer, whom I'm dealing with right now, want?
- Consult your customers on a regular basis, through simple communication (emails, letters, pamphlets) or via surveys and focus groups.
- Use mystery shopping and mirror customer behaviour.
- Establish your customers' moments of truth.

Examples

- Heathrow Terminal Five held trial customer check-in and baggage days, but when they took the terminal 'live', they had well-documented failures, many of which involved simple customer service issues such as the training of staff in how to direct customers in the building and the collection and transportation of customer baggage from check-in to aircraft in time for their flight. Avoid upsetting your customers in this way.
- Orange, the mobile phone business, uses an automated 'best package tracker', and their advisers use every contact to refine and update customer profiles with their latest needs. Is your company capable of delivering this level of service to your customers?
- Sainsbury's use complaints as an opportunity to 'walk the store' with a customer to understand how they shop and what they look out for. Can your business provide something similar?
- Avis used a cultural training programme to cut complaints and improve service. Could this be an effective technique in your business?
- Harley-Davidson builds a community of customers and advocates to understand them better. Would the same approach work for your organization?

2

Great customer service and experience

The basics

In this chapter we will seek to identify what great service is – and how the concept of customer experience applies to your business.

> *Is customer experience the new customer battleground that will determine today's business winners and losers, or is it simply a new interpretation of great customer service?*

This question is one you need to answer on behalf of your organization in order to clarify your strategic approach to this area. This chapter aims to help you answer that question.

The introduction to BS 8477 states that:

> The relationship between the customer or consumer and the organizations providing them with products and services has never been more in focus – and critical to the success of those organizations. The customer service professional – whether in a frontline role such as a retail assistant, call centre service adviser or client account manager, or in a management role such as call centre manager or customer service director – has never been more important.

Maintaining or improving upon customer satisfaction levels is one of the most important contributing factors in the running of a successful organization in any sector. *Harvard Business Review* (Nov–Dec 1995 and September 2009) summarized the business benefits as the '3Rs': retention, related sales and referrals. According to research by the Institute of Customer Service, customers perceive the following elements as being the most important in service delivery: timeliness, appearance, courtesy, quality and efficiency, ease of doing business and problem solving. These elements might be summarized as another set of '3Rs' that apply equally in the commercial and the public sectors, where commercial imperatives are often less pressing: responsiveness, reliability and respect.

So customer service and satisfaction levels have never been more important, but defining what this means to customers has never been easy – especially in today's technology-driven and fast-moving business world.

Pine and Gilmore (1998) first introduced the concept of customer experience in 1998, stating that the next competitive battleground for leading-edge companies 'lies in staging experiences'. They recognized the emerging experience economy that was beginning to shape the transition from businesses selling services to businesses selling experiences. According to their analysis, an experience is 'not an amorphous construct; it is as real an offering as any service, good, or commodity' (Pine and Gilmore, 1998).

Thompson and Kolsky (2004) define an experience 'as the sum total of conscious events' and go on to state that experiences 'involve all five senses' as well as being both a relational and an emotional event – therefore businesses must act accordingly.[2]

Furthermore, it has been shown that a customer's perception of an organization is built as a result of their interaction across multiple channels and that a positive customer experience can result in an increased share of wallet and repeat business. The following chart from a 2009 consumer survey shows how exceeding customer expectations can improve spend with the business.

If the business exceeds my expectations, my annual spending with this business will:

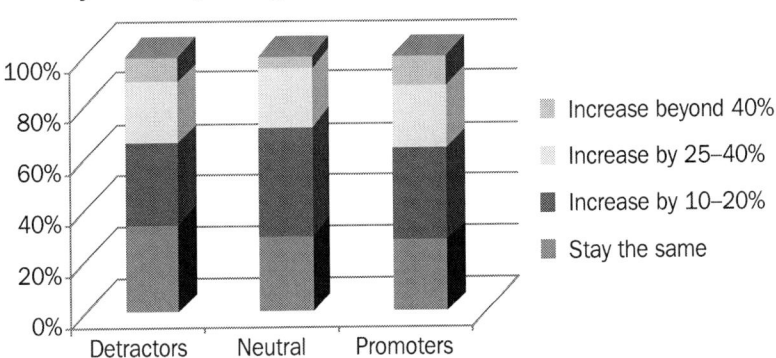

	Detractors	Neutral	Promoters
Increase beyond 40%			
Increase by 25–40%			
Increase by 10–20%			
Stay the same			

Figure 3. Strativity Group 2009 Customer Experience Consumer Study: consumers pay for exceptional customer experiences

---

[2] This research does not necessarily reflect Gartner's current view of the marketplace and should be viewed in historical terms.

So, the concept of customer experience is relatively new in comparison to the practice of customer service, which has existed for centuries. Customer experience is certainly the most talked about and written about concept in the service world. But in fact all it is doing is simply evolving the way we define what the industry regards as great customer service in today's world. This evolution is, however, important, as it reflects the growing demand of customers for more and better service.

The counter-argument is that it is vey unlikely that most customers are looking for an 'experience' at any stage of their day. Take the example of Jane in Chapter 1. Jane is a busy working woman whose core need is fast, efficient service to give her what she wants or needs.

This is why understanding your customer is so critical, as it will determine which of the customer groupings that your organization serves are liable to respond best to an evolved customer service 'experience'. That evolved experience for Jane is probably best represented by her interaction with the station kiosk, where the assistant had recognized her need for speed and efficiency and pre-prepared her order so that all she needed to do was pay and dash for her train.

In other customer groupings, where speed is not necessarily the overarching requirement, you will have more scope to enhance the 'experience' in a way that helps you to develop the customer's relationship with you, and hence their loyalty to your organization and products or services.

Chris Voss (London Business School) has long had a reputation as an expert in this area and has written a number of research papers. He observes that attention to the customer experience is becoming increasingly important to UK organizations. Voss surveyed UK FTSE100 businesses, and results indicated that four out of five respondents believed that customer experience was very important to them and their business and that they would be placing more emphasis on it in the future because of the identified premium pricing and customer retention implications (Kakkad and Voss, 2006). He comments, however, that this has not been reflected in most organizations by giving specific responsibility for customer experience to any individual. Where that person did exist – more usually in B2C than B2B businesses – they reported at board level (Kakkad and Voss, 2006).

One of the drivers for the attention on customer experience is the decline of traditional media and customer interactions and the rise of new media and the embedding of technology as part of the fabric or delivery of so many products and services. A classic example is that of the ATM bank system, where only a few people now go to a teller window to draw out cash from their account.

New media and technology driven services and their use in the design and delivery of customer service will be covered in more depth in Chapter 6, but it is important at this stage to recognize that the rise of the internet, services driven and delivered by technology and social media have changed the customer service landscape – for ever.

Chris Voss's report *Trusting the Internet: Developing an eService Strategy* (commissioned by the Institute of Customer Service in 2000) featured the fundamental building block 'pyramid of service'.

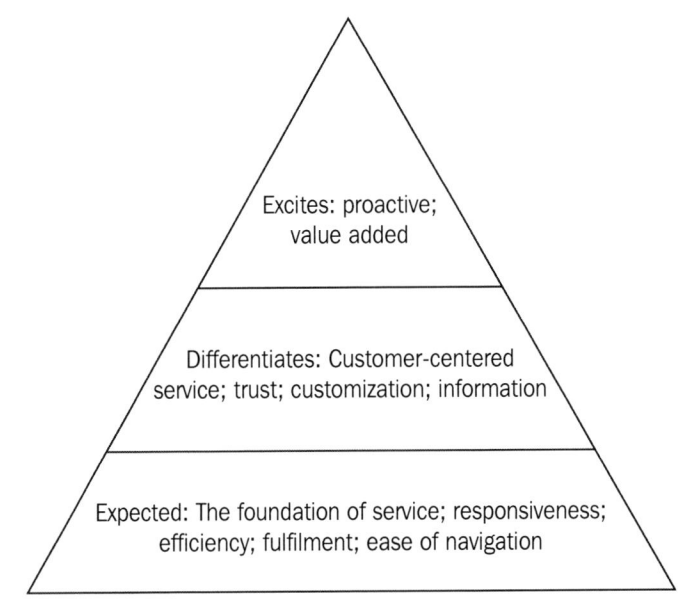

Figure 4. Pyramid of service (Words extracted from Voss (2000), diagram by Howard Kendall (2009).

This is fundamental to any service offer – in any service environment – because it covers every aspect of great customer service and integrates the customer experience concept in the excitement pinnacle of the pyramid. To achieve great customer service, you must first establish a firm foundation that is responsive, efficient and fulfils customer requirements. You then need to become customer centered to differentiate your service from that of others by building trust and offering customized service with extra information. Finally, you need to add an excitement factor to the customer experience, most likely by being proactive and anticipating needs and desires.

In their report, *Customer Priorities: What Customers Really Want* (2006), Nigel Hill and Stephen Hampshire make the following observation:

> Customers will tend to reward companies that satisfy them and punish those that do not. This fundamentally influences the way free markets operate, driving organizations to deliver as much customer satisfaction as they can in the most efficient way possible. This phenomenon has been strengthened by the growing power of customers based on their higher levels of education and confidence plus, in recent years, dramatically increased sources of information, resulting in the production-led economies of the past turning into today's customer-driven markets. There is also growing evidence that today's affluent consumer in developed economies has become more interested in quality of life (doing things) than material wealth (owning things). This further reinforces the importance of the entire customer experience, not just the core product or service. (Hill and Hampshire, 2006)

This quote also introduces a further dimension – that of the customer punishing the organization that does not deliver basic levels of customer satisfaction. We will deal with the success and failure of customer service in Chapter 7, but it is useful to indicate the types of customer service experience that will cause customer punishment. Hill and Hampshire's research indicates that the most common were:

- broken promises (including the failure to phone back);
- remoteness of human contact;
- refusal to apologize (even when the service supplier has clearly made an error);
- failure to empathize with the distress of the customer;
- processes and systems that are not customer friendly;
- 'corporate arrogance';
- a reluctance to welcome complaints.

This gives rise, of course, to the requirement for organizations to avoid the negative conditions above and if they do occur, to react positively and re-establish the customer's trust and confidence. We will be covering this at length in subsequent chapters, and there is excellent guidance in BS ISO 10002 *Customer satisfaction – Guidelines for complaints handling in organizations*.

The customer experience

The early part of this chapter has dealt with positioning the concept of the customer experience relative to the fundamentals of customer service. An outstanding customer experience forms the pinnacle of the pyramid and should be the 'vision' that organizations aspire to achieve when considering customer service strategy.

We will now go on to consider which factors might influence the definition of great customer service or experiences:

- age or generation;
- geography, nationality or culture;
- B2B;
- consistency from third parties or multiple outlets;
- emotion;
- brand loyalty.

Each of these factors has unique issues to understand or to address and build on the understanding of customers established in Chapter 1. To start to imagine what might constitute a great customer experience in real terms, let us consider these examples of businesses and venues built to appeal to 'experience-seekers':

- The O_2 arena in Greenwich, London, now the world's leading live music and events venue, has built a whole village of smaller theatres, bars, restaurants and a cinema around it to offer a complete leisure experience for many different customer groups. Added to the entertainment mix is easy access by public transport or car and regular email information services to offer both guidance and advance notice of coming events.
- Decathlon, the French sports retailer, has built its stores to offer a wide range of sporting goods and clothing, both branded and own brand, in an environment where you can try out your tennis racket or golf clubs in a 'test before you buy' area.
- Nike stores cater for their younger and more style-conscious sports clothing buyers with contemporary store designs and layouts, making their stores a place to hang out in rather than just to buy sports gear.
- Waterstone's (and now other bookstores) have long offered coffee bars and sofa areas for customers to browse through the books they might be interested in buying, resulting in an 'experience' designed to keep customers in the store for longer.

- Mercedes-Benz World in Brooklands, Surrey, has a museum, track and off-road driving experiences, a conference centre, restaurant and children's events to add to the standard showroom experience of selecting your car.

Van Boven and Gilovich (2003) proved the long-held maxim that experiences contribute more to long-term life satisfaction than do material possessions. Other studies had shown that when the basic needs of food, shelter, etc. are met, extra material wealth does not lead to greater happiness across countries. This study further showed that individual consumption of *experiential* purchases led to greater satisfaction than did material purchases. The authors advance three potential explanations for this finding:

- Experiences may be more favourably viewed as time passes.
- Experiences are more central to one's identity.
- Experiences have greater social value (in other words they are more interesting to talk about).

The implications of this study are that, as customers, we should look to use our discretionary spend on experiential purchases where possible and that, as suppliers, we should try to sell experiences not products.

Service by generation

If you combine the demographics of the population and the divergence of behaviour and attitudes depending on age range, it represents a truly seismic shift in customer behaviour and requirements. Jane's 'need for speed' aligns closely with the typical service needs and desires of young professionals today. If you keep them waiting – either in a queue or by expecting them to make too many clicks to get to the right part of your website – you run a serious risk of losing them. They might not be too bothered about high degrees of politeness or 'service with a smile'. When these customers are in what they regard as 'leisure mode' – when they are looking for entertainment or purchases relating to fashion, music or sport – they may well demand a more superior experience. If you are able to achieve this, purchases will tend to be both impulsive and instant.

Alternatively, consider the service needs of 50–70 year olds. This age range has become the new middle age and will be where the 'grey market' of affluent older consumers with significant disposable incomes and more time will hold the key to the success of many businesses. Although they may make less impulsive buys, many will spend more per transaction as they may well have paid off mortgages, collected redundancy or pension payments or simply have fewer outgoings than a growing family. They will be doubly demanding, though, in insisting on an excellent customer service and experience. Because they will probably have researched before the purchase, they will be more interested in a great deal than are many younger customers. This older group still requires 'old-fashioned' politeness and courtesy alongside whatever purchase they make and will increasingly be the first 'tech-savvy' older generation.

Some examples of businesses built to appeal to older customers are given below.

- *Polhill Garden Centre (Sevenoaks, Kent).* This business has thrived for 30 years while many similar chains have faltered. It mixes shopping experiences, offering an in-house butcher, cake shop, small supermarket and greengrocer. Their restaurant features tea dances and jazz lunches, and there are coach trips and historically themed events in the grounds too.
- *McCarthy & Stone.* This organization has long offered tailored retirement or assisted living housing to older citizens, and over 90 per cent of customers 'recommend a friend'.
- *Saga.* Saga is well known as a specialist 'older brand' and offers a full range of services from help with care or independent living to product offerings for money, health and holidays.

In the past, the 70 years and over age group has been seen as a problem to be solved, rather than as an opportunity to seize. Today we have the chance to offer this group the same range of tailored services or experiences that we would offer to a younger audience. Life expectancy at birth in the UK has reached its highest level on record for both males and females. A newborn boy can expect to live 77.2 years and a newborn girl to 81.5 years (Office of National Statistics (ONS), 2009). An official government study has shown that, for the first time, there are more pensioners than children under 16 in the UK (ONS, 2009). We need to get used to the fact that most of our customers are part of an ageing population.

This older customer community will expect the same politeness and courtesy as 50–70 year olds, but they will not be quite as tech savvy. That, in itself, offers an opportunity to provide a service to this generation – teaching them to use the internet, for example, will open a whole new world to them that they may never have experienced before.

The growing percentage of older consumers, estimated as 21 million over-50s (Mintel, 2009), will increasingly demand great service and different customer experiences, and there is currently a lack of understanding and research on what they will actually want. It is safe to assume, however, that many will have time and money on their hands and will be looking to take advantage of that position. We need to consider that in our future service offerings. For example, many of my own friends are using the internet to research senior housing options for their parents. Tomorrow, these same friends will explore their own senior living choices.

Industry professionals need to adapt their advertising and marketing strategies to the practices of today's consumers and tomorrow's retiring population. It is very noticeable that older generations seem to be 'invisible' to advertisers, who primarily target younger consumers. A recent US study of internet usage showed that online access for older web surfers is close to doubling over three years (Jones and Fox, 2009). Their surfing leans much more toward accessing factual information relating to health and government issues rather than to the entertainment drive of younger surfers. For the advertisers and service providers that recognize this, there is a huge opportunity to build a larger customer base.

Generational differences in internet use

Compared with teens and Generation Y, older generations use the internet less for socializing and entertainment and more as a tool for information searches, emailing and buying products. In particular, older internet users are significantly more likely than younger users to look online for health information. Health questions drive internet users aged 73 and older to the internet just as frequently as they drive Generation Y users, outpacing teens by a significant margin. Researching health information is the third most popular online activity with the most senior age group, after email and online searching.

Internet users aged 33–72 years are also significantly more likely than younger users to look online for religious information and are more likely to visit government websites to search for information (Jones and Fox, 2009).

Service by nationality, geography or culture

The service requirements of different nations or cultures were looked at briefly in Chapter 1, but understanding what constitutes great service for each different customer group is fundamental to meeting their needs.

Understanding and acting on cultural or geographical differences can affect attitudes and behaviour sufficiently to make your customer service operation either succeed or fail, which is why there is an investment by many multinational corporations in understanding different market cultures and expectations. The Harley-Davidson example in Chapter 1 is an excellent illustration of this.

An Accenture report, *Leadership in Customer Service: Delivering on the Promise* (2007), examines the provision of service to citizens in a range of countries, and unsurprisingly the often highlighted Singapore leads the rankings of countries in terms of customer service maturity. The report highlights the differences in cultural approaches to customer service. For example, Anabela Pedroso, president of Portugal's Agency for Public Services Reform, refers to the desire of the Portuguese Government to deliver service to customers in the way Amazon operates online, by knowing what the customer might want this time because you have learnt what they did/bought last time (Accenture, 2007).

In marked contrast, Christophe Alviset, under-director of information and new technologies at France's Ministry of Economy, Finance and Industry, describes the prevailing attitude in his country this way: 'We're not that inclined to think in a customer service way. And I'm not sure that clients expect it that much either. They're used to how the administration behaves. They're not surprised. What they want is a more streamlined administration, but they're not demanding to have a single access' (Accenture, 2007).

It is clear from these examples that market cultures and expectations will significantly define what great service is for different customer segments and will require constant monitoring and product/service evolution.

Service for B2B

The differentiation of service between businesses, B2B, rather than from a business to a consumer, B2C, is quite dangerous in my view. It implies that perhaps the fundamental principles of service should be different for business customers. As shown in Jane's example in Chapter 1, the design agency simply did not meet her delivery expectations. This is no different from delivering to a consumer, and the need for a good product also prevails. My advice is, therefore, to maintain the same service principles as for consumers but to recognize that business deadlines may sharpen the need to hit delivery times promptly. Understanding the businesses you supply to, and their business drivers and deadlines, will generally ensure long-term loyalty if you consistently meet their needs. Businesses value consistent, reliable service above all.

To understand other businesses, it is worth examining your own businesses' moments of truth, which will very likely be similar to those of many other organizations. Great service is likely to involve building a relationship with customers over a longer buying cycle, or it may be delivering an instant solution to solve an immediate business problem. See, for example, the case of Viking Direct, as noted on page 8.

B2B services, and hence their customer expectation of 'great service', can range from the simple office supplies example on page 8 to the highly complex such as the order of specialized scientific or medical devices. In the former case it is enough to meet the previously stated requirement to hit, or beat, delivery expectations with a good-quality product. In the latter case this approach is likely to be insufficient. In a complex sale there will be an expectation from the customer that the supplier will seek to build a relationship with them, to learn their needs over a long period of time and tailor products and services to fit their needs accurately.

One of the most prominent B2B services is that of managed services. This can simply be IT services that are to be outsourced to a specialist supplier or can accommodate all the services that an organization needs to carry out its business – buildings, logistics, transport, staff, IT. One of the principal aims for businesses that are interested in managed services is to achieve the same or improved levels of service at a consistently lower cost. It would be impossible, therefore, to sell to a client and give them the service they need without an in-depth understanding of the client and their business.

A key issue for B2B service is to understand what has been sold to customers and what promises have been made to them and, therefore, what expectations have been set. A perennial problem for organizations is that salespersons have often not listened to specific customer needs, and there is a mismatch between what has been sold and what can effectively be delivered. Nowhere has this been more visible than in the IT-managed service/outsourcing market where several high-profile cases have hit the newspapers when the relationship has broken down. Two such examples from Martin (2007) illustrate the point. The HM Revenue & Customs (HMRC) tax credits system, where HMRC has tried both Electronic Data Systems (EDS) and Cap Gemini as suppliers, has paid out over £300m, and they still do not have a website that works properly. As a result, the credits system has already had to write off £1.4bn in overpayments. Sainsbury's 'Business Transformation Programme' used Accenture as a supplier to deliver a new stock system – and apparently it could not track stock. Sainsbury's lost £550m of profits and had to draft in 3,000 new shelf stackers at short notice. Accenture responded by blaming Sainsbury's for insufficient due diligence (Martin, 2007).

In addition to the fundamental observation that the service team needs to be involved early in the sales cycle for such services, the organization should ensure that staff in all roles have a basic ability to understand and interpret customer requirements.

In the Institute of Customer Service research paper *Excellence in Managing the Business-to-Business Customer Relationship* (Institute of Customer Service, 2007), customers who felt that their suppliers were providing a good service in a B2B relationship identified the following common traits:

- They take ownership and deal with things.
- They tend to be in tune with the way the business is going and have a reasonable handle on what we expect from them.
- There is consistency in service, consistency in approach, consistency in price and consistency in the people.
- They meet targets and expectations.
- They bring added value, rather than just doing the job.

(Institute of Customer Service, 2007)

For the suppliers who provided the worst service, the traits were as follows:

- Simple courtesies are not always present.
- There is a lack of respect for who they are dealing with.
- There is a lack of openness, honesty and directness in supplier dealings.
- They hide behind legislation rather than solving the problem.
- They have an inflexible approach to organizational culture and business practices.
- They lack flexible long-term development plans and are unable to adapt to change.

(Institute of Customer Service, 2007)

The worst practices were often linked to named individuals. Failure to deliver was more consistently attributed to employees rather than to the systems in place; however, in reality, the causal factors should be attributed more to the way that human resources of the supplier are managed.

Service consistency – third parties and multiple outlets

From a customer perspective, a brand that has given good service in one location must be able to deliver consistently in other locations to avoid losing its loyal customers. In the box overleaf are testimonials from two customers of the budget hi-fi and TV chain, Richer Sounds, which has long had a reputation for great service.

> 'Brilliant, superb and amazing. 1st class customer service, advice and value. Julian Richer tries to get customers for life and he certainly has that from myself. I have never heard a bad thing said about Richer Sounds. Julian Richer is a big advocate of customer service and his books on how to run a company are superb and a must read for any business owner. It certainly shows when you go to Richer Sounds that he practices what he preaches.' (Qype, 2009)
>
> 'I cannot say enough good things about Richer Sounds. Although the [Edinburgh] shop is tiny, the stock is quality. We have bought TVs, DVD players, video recorders, Freeview boxes and HIFIs here. The staff are great and will help you into the car with large purchases. It's worth subscribing to the email alerts because you will get special offers and free stuff. We got free headphones only just recently. They always have good 'managers specials' on stock, so pop in regularly. My brother recently got £200 off a plasma telly because it was the last one. I never have any bother returning stuff either.' (Qype, 2009)

These are impressive testimonials for a small chain that specializes in finding cheap, edge-of-town stores and then piling them high with stock. Because customers do not expect plush premises, Richer Sounds ensures that its staff is knowledgeable, well trained and incentivized to give great service.

Another area in which it can be difficult to maintain consistency is where you do not control all of the moments of truth in your customer's experience of your business because some elements are delivered by third parties. This might be because you have chosen to outsource them to a specialist, such as a logistics supplier, or because you have little choice, such as in the airline business where you cannot choose the airport at which you are based.

The customer might have bought the product or service from you and expects your standards, but having selected the third party, you are dependent on them to live up to your service promise. This makes both the selection process, and the ongoing management of their delivery of your product, critical. The selection process should be just as rigorous as when you select an internal team.

Emotion

Alongside the rise in popularity of the customer experience there has been a similar rise in the focus on satisfying the emotional needs of customers, largely due to the mounting weight of evidence that emotional spend enhances customer loyalty.

Lior Arussy is an author, visionary, consultant and creative catalyst. He is a pioneer of CEM (customer experience management) and received *CRM Magazine*'s '2003 Influential Leaders' award for his thought leadership and contribution to the customer experience industry. He wrote in his customer experience column on MyCustomer.com in 2009: 'We recently conducted a study among 1,994 consumers in the US and Canada. The purpose of the study was to discover if customer loyalty is dead due to the challenging economic conditions that most consumers currently face. The report revealed that customers are paying careful attention to the experiences they receive from companies with whom they conduct business, and are rewarding or penalizing those companies accordingly' (Arussy, 2009). Some pertinent findings include the following:

- *Share of wallet*: over two-thirds of consumers indicate that they are willing to spend 10 per cent or more with businesses if those businesses exceed their expectations.
- *Customer retention*: loyal customers are almost three times as likely to expect to continue doing business with companies for another 10 years or more than are dissatisfied customers. Dissatisfied customers are 10 times more likely to defect in the next twelve months than are their loyal counterparts.
- *Pay more*: 40 per cent of loyal customers said that they were willing to pay 10 per cent or more to continue purchasing from companies delivering great experiences. In contrast, only nine per cent of dissatisfied customers are willing to spend more with those companies.
(Arussy, 2009)

In determining a 'great experience', customers are clear about what they are seeking from the experiences businesses deliver. They are, generally:

- quick and effective issue resolution;
- common sense and discretion;
- employees who exceed expectations;
- ease and simplicity of transaction.

Customer emotions are driven much more by how the staff treats customers than by the technical or functional quality of the product or service. Have we moved to a designer service phase where ordinary goods are moving into designer territory not through the cost or quality of the product but through the service or experience around them?

A great product can be destroyed by a rude employee, and a commoditized product can be made great by an employee going beyond the call of duty in pursuit of delivering great customer service, making the customer experience more personal, more positive and more memorable.

Furthermore, by connecting with the employees, the customers are connecting with the brand or the organization, which increases customer loyalty. To that end, several experienced service providers hire employees based on empathic skills (or emotional intelligence). These skills refer to the ability to perceive and assess your own emotions and those of others.

For example, Luminar Leisure recognized the importance of the 'people element' for a pleasant night out and has started to train the frontline employees of both their Lava & Ignite and Liquid nightclubs in empathic skills. As part of this training, door staff are taught to recognize different customer segments and respond to them with a response tailored to that particular person.

Other businesses, known as 'emotional winners', have a strong emotional pull. Consider the examples below:

- Virgin Atlantic, the flagship airline business of Richard Branson's brand empire, has long had a loyal customer following. It achieves the indefinable 'buzz' that keeps customers returning. Its premium cabins – and especially the Heathrow upper-class lounge – excel and stand out across the industry.
- first direct, the phone and online bank, ensures that each customer transaction is handled personally by an adviser with a target of achieving a win–win result in even the most difficult customer interactions.

Emotional intelligence (often referred to as EQ or 'emotional quotient') is a recent behavioural model, highlighted in Daniel Goleman's book, *Emotional Intelligence* (1995). Emotional intelligence is increasingly relevant to organizational development and developing people, because the EQ principles provide a new way to understand and assess people's behaviours, management styles, attitudes, interpersonal skills and potential. These are, of course, key in establishing relationships with customers.

Brand loyalty

Often regarded as the 'holy grail' outcome of good service to customers, brand loyalty incorporates and builds on many of the previous areas such as emotion and generational considerations.

Branding has long been a marketing strategy to provide organizations with an identity in line with their offering. Whether large or small, your organization is a brand even if you have not given a moment's thought to what it should represent. Consider this definition:

> A brand is a *promise*. It encapsulates what people think about your business, product or service when they encounter it:

- What do they think your brand offers?
- Is their understanding of your brand what you wish it to be?
- How is your 'offer' differentiated from that of your competitors?
- Do people *trust* your brand to deliver that offer?
- What *personality* do they attribute to it?
- How does their perception alter once they have bought from you?

(New Brand Experience: Branding Fundamentals, 2009)

The product or service you offer, together with how you offer and deliver it, all contribute to your brand image. Google is a famous brand in its own right, delivering an indispensible internet search engine service to millions of customers. There are several other search engines available, but 'to Google' is the only one that has made it into the dictionary and become part of everyday language. Much of that achievement comes from the ease of access and use that Google has developed and the consistency of the service.

Brands, and the loyalty they attract, are an inescapable feature of 21st century B2C and B2B environments. The way they can influence the emotions of a customer and induce them to spend more with an organization, remain loyal over a longer period and even pay a premium price is reason enough to ensure that they will remain so.

A particularly unique kind of organization in this respect is the football (soccer) club. It is almost impossible for a football club to lose customers if the team remains reasonably successful. Clubs are often said to exploit the emotion their supporters have for their team (brand) with everything from expensive tickets and replica kit to selling premium-priced pies at matches. It takes a lot to drive these customers away, and if club owners listen sensibly to the supporters, they can avoid loss of fans.

Other fine examples of the familiar B2C brands to which customers readily identify themselves as loyal followers are Disney, Virgin, first direct bank and Apple. They do not always get everything right, but the strength of the brand allows them to fail occasionally, and as long as they recover well, they retain the loyalty of their customers.

As an example, several colleagues, customers and I were marooned for two days in Orlando by Virgin Atlantic. An electrical fault had grounded the plane, and the fault reoccurred the following day just as we were about to take off, despite assurances that it had been fixed.

This was a major incident in customer service terms and affected hundreds of passengers. It was handled badly in Orlando, with poor communication and terrible local customer care and recovery methods. As a result, we submitted a detailed complaint to CEO Steve Ridgway on our eventual return. Virgin subsequently invited us to participate in their post-mortem of the event and listened to our account of what happened. As a result, Virgin changed their technical delay processes to ensure that nothing like this happened again. In addition to crediting our accounts with enough loyalty miles for further free US return flights, this type of response has kept me as a loyal customer up to the present day.

B2B brands identified in the book *Business Superbrands 2009* with similarly trusted profiles include Chubb (locks and security), Sodexo and Compass (catering and building facilities), Microsoft and Sony (technology) and BP and Michelin (fuels and automotive).

Research by Professor Voss at the London Business School (*Experience and the Brand*, 2005) highlights the clear links between the delivery of great customer experiences and brand loyalty. The strategic use of experience for customers at branded destinations such as Bluewater in Kent, the Guinness Storehouse in Dublin, Hamley's toystore in London and Legoland near Windsor have all developed loyalty to their brands in the respective customer portfolios.

Summary

At the beginning of this chapter I promised to identify what great service is and how the concept of customer experience applies to your business. I also suggested that you need to answer the following question for your organization:

> *Is customer experience the new customer battleground that will determine today's business winners and losers, or simply the new interpretation of great customer service?*

In this chapter, I have established for you what great service is. The positioning of the customer experience at the pinnacle of the pyramid of service should also be clear. As you develop your thoughts on how your organization should apply these, the factors of age or generation, geography, nationality or culture, B2B, consistency from third parties or multiple outlets, emotion and brand loyalty should also be considered.

Learning points

This chapter has built on the start point of customer service in Chapter 1 where we established that understanding your customer's basic needs and desires from the product or service you have to offer is crucial to being able to develop your customer service offering. In order to establish great service and to offer customers a customer experience that will achieve customer satisfaction, loyalty and increased spend there are several points to remember:

- Understand the basic structure of customer service – from the service pyramid foundation of responsiveness, efficiency and fulfilment through the customer-centred approach to build trust, customize services and add valuable information, to the final customer experience development pinnacle of proactive and value-added service.
- Understand and track your performance in your key moments of truth where you have the chance to succeed or fail in the customer's perception. It is much easier to prevent the customer punishing you for poor products or service if you understand what constitutes great service to your customers.
- Understand how the factors of age or generation, geography, nationality or culture, B2B, consistency from third parties or multiple outlets, emotion and brand loyalty affect your customers.
- Understand in particular the emotional connection that your customer has with your brand. If you have this, you really want to keep it; if not, you really want to build it.

Shaun Smith, of www.smithcoconsultancy.com, who has worked with many of the world's leading brands, has offered his top 10 tips for managing your customer experience:

1. Leaders must be actively and continually involved.
2. HR, operations and marketing must own it.
3. Focus on your most strategically important customers.
4. Find out what these customers truly value.
5. Design CEM before designing your CRM system.

6. Use customer experience to retain customers rather than attempting to lock them in via so-called loyalty cards.
7. Communicate to your people before your customers.
8. Create differentiated training for your people.
9. Measure and reward those activities and behaviours that drive the desired customer experience.
10. Measure customer experience rather than satisfaction.

(Smith, 2009)

Smith & co. observes that execution is the most difficult part of creating the branded customer experience – these points will help to guide you.

The following is a short list of techniques and examples to consider and learn from.

Techniques:

- Study successful organizations for indications of how they succeed with service that you can replicate in your own business.
- Study unsuccessful organizations and figure out what they did wrong so that you do not make the same mistakes.
- Use the influencing factors in this chapter – age/generation, geography/culture, B2B or B2C, emotion and brand – to tune your customer service model.
- Avoid customer punishment through poor service: it is corrosive to your brand reputation. Investing in a customer solution that may seem expensive at the time will be worthwhile in the longer term in enhancing customer retention and lifetime spending with you. The Nokia Siemens 'avoidance of churn' featured in Chapter 1 aims to do exactly this.
- Build your own customer pyramid. Consider offering premium customers better levels of service while still meeting foundation levels at lower spend levels.
- Use the *Harvard Business Review* '3 Rs' of retention, related sales and referrals, to guide and track the success of your service offer, supplemented by the parallel '3 Rs' from the Institute of Customer Service of responsiveness, reliability and respect.

Examples:

- There are inspirational examples throughout this book and in the recommended reading, but to study for consistency over the life of their businesses, both first direct and Virgin Atlantic, the latter having just celebrated their 25th anniversary, have successfully dominated their fields in sustained service/brand reputation.

It is much more difficult to keep great service going – these two companies have succeeded through commitment, focus and continual innovation and improvement.
- Further afield, Disney and the other theme park operators have made it their business to continually innovate with the service that surrounds their rides and attractions, for example the management and entertainment of queues.
- In the UK, the O$_2$ arena and Mercedes-Benz-World have brought additional 'experience' services to bear to add to their core product offering.

3

Customer service strategy, culture and objectives

A great service model

Having already discussed the importance of understanding the customer and having analysed what great service is, we will establish in this chapter how your organization can achieve consistently great service to your customers. This will include both strategic and tactical areas of focus that will help you to achieve a resilient business model for service, which is essential for the consistent delivery that all service-led organizations should strive for.

A 2008 report from the Institute of Customer Service, *World-Class Customer Service*, uses the following model:

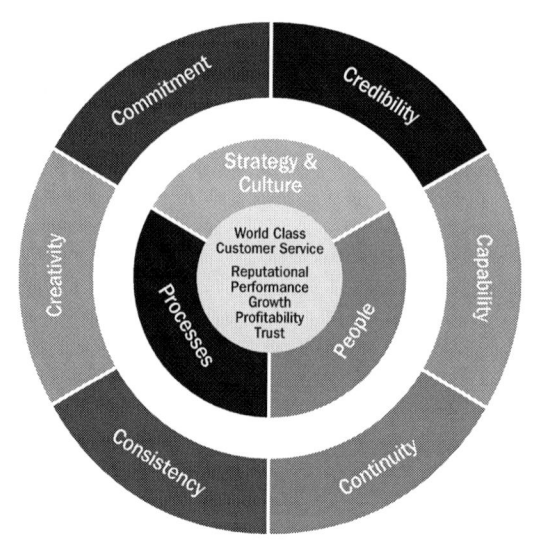

Figure 5. World-Class Customer Service (Institute of Customer Service, 2008).

The model defines the attributes of reputation, performance, growth, profitability and trust at its core. It suggests that commitment and credibility should be key parts of strategy and culture in the organization, processes should be creative and consistent, and that continuity and staff capability should be addressed in order to provide world-class customer service. Its major achievement, however, is demonstrating the requirement to develop a business model for service that is appropriate for your organization and customers and that is flexible and resilient.

In this chapter we will establish the key areas of focus and the 'road map' for the successful development of *your* model. Although it will, of course, comment on the strategic elements of people, processes and technology, these are so crucial to your success that each of these has a chapter of its own later in the book.

Before you start

There are two essential questions to answer before you start to prepare your customer service business model:

- What level of service does your organization want – or need – to achieve?
- What are your competitors, other comparable businesses and businesses you admire doing and what can you adapt to fit your model?

The first question should be relatively simple for you to answer. The best way to illustrate the second question, though, is by examining the airline industry. Some of the longer-established airlines, such as British Airways, American Airlines, United Airlines and Lufthansa, are losing customers to the newer budget carriers such as easyJet, Ryanair, Kingfisher and AirAsia.

The big advantage that these new carriers have is the lack of a legacy of cost – because of huge overheads such as pension funds, large staff establishments and capital infrastructures that restrict the ability to change, at least quickly – that the older airlines carry. Perhaps an even bigger advantage is that they are able to choose where to position their flight and service in relation to today's cost-conscious business and leisure travel markets.

Some airlines have chosen to augment the basic service of getting you from A to B with exceptional service at a premium price; for example the new first-class suite in a Singapore Airlines (SIA) A380 plane from London to Singapore will cost you just over £7,000 return (price for September 2009) and yet it is possible to fly the same journey for under £500 in an economy seat or to fly from London to

Dublin or Paris for well under £100 if you book ahead. These lower price levels were unthinkable 10 years ago – and have forced competition onto what was perceived to be a quite 'comfortable' industry.

The point is that today, levels of service below what we would consider acceptable have become acceptable if the price is right. Michael O'Leary has continually sought to promote Ryanair as the 'if you don't like it, spend more to fly with someone else' airline (my words not his!) but it remains one of the most profitable airlines, with a good record for reliability and a loyal customer base. Charges for food, checking in at the airport, and putting a bag in the hold, and poor customer complaint resolution have all failed to put off customers. They continue to book with Ryanair, proving the point that it is possible to sell what many consider to be a poor offering if 'the price is right'.

Before you start, therefore, evaluate what will form the philosophy behind your service strategy – is it to deliver a highly price-competitive offer that has only basic levels of service included, or is it to deliver a superior customer experience at a premium price? Remember the learning point from Chapter 1 – what does this customer, whom I'm dealing with right now, want?

There is an endless quest for the holy grail of ever-improving service, but can your business – and its customers – afford it? If not, or the customers are unwilling to pay for anything beyond it, then it is perfectly acceptable to deliver a foundation level of service.

Help from standards

There is a wide selection of standards on which you can draw to help you establish what key elements you should include in your customer service model. BS ISO 9001 states that 'top management shall ensure that customer requirements are determined and are met with the aim of enhancing customer satisfaction'. It is a very simple statement but it encapsulates the ethos behind the customer service strategy. Other standards offering help to define the essentials for your model are: BS 8477, which offers guidance on a range of aspects of customer service best practice, but especially customer service principles and obligations for all levels of the organization. This book will reference these publications frequently: BS ISO 10002, offering guidance on the management of complaints; Institute of Customer Service Servicemark, which extends the world-class model referred to earlier and offers guidance on building elements such as commitment, credibility and capability; and *Customer Service Excellence*, the UK Government standard issued by the Cabinet Office, which offers guidance in all areas but is particularly relevant for customer satisfaction and feedback, leadership and culture and staff attributes.

These standards are the best 'general' customer services standards available. Standards form a vital backdrop to the commercial application of customer service best practice, in addition to being an excellent benchmark to check your model for completeness. There are standards available in specific areas of customer service, for example the Contact Centre Association and BSI have specific standards for contact centres, the Service Desk Institute for IT service desks and the British Hospitality Association for hotels and restaurants. Although it is possible to find and often independently certify your organization against standards in almost every area of service, you should make sure that you are selecting the most appropriate and complete standard for your particular need.

The project plan

For any new project for implementation, or for an update to existing processes or products, and whatever the size of your organization, you will require a plan. This book is not a project management publication so it will not give detailed advice but BSI has two standards in the area – BS ISO 10006:2003 and BS ISO 10007:2003. The well-known PRINCE2 project management methodology also provides guidance (http://www.prince2.com/what-is-prince2.asp).

The scale of the project plan you develop should be in proportion to the size of your operation and the scope of the project – if you are a small builder or garden service company setting up a simple, practical customer service model, your plan might be less than a page and take a few hours or days to construct and implement. If you are a large multinational business it may be several pages long and take several months or more to implement.

BS 8477 advises that having a senior person with responsibility, authority and preferably a high degree of passion and commitment to lead the project is essential, and that the assembly of, and consultation with, a steering group made up of managers, frontline service staff and customers provides stakeholder opinion, guidance and support at the crucial early stages and throughout the implementation.

The role of strategy, culture and policies

The 2008 National Business Awards identified the hosting service provider Rackspace as having the best customer focus in the UK. Rackspace has developed core values to reflect the importance of customer service in its culture:

- fanatical support in all we do;
- results first; substance over flash;
- embrace change for excellence;
- passion in our work;
- keep our promises;
- treat fellow 'Rackers' (Rackspace employees) like friends and family.

(Rackspace, 2009)

For customers, fanatical support means that Rackspace employees are available 24–7–365 to meet and exceed customers' expectations. Every customer gets a fast response to critical issues, unlimited technical phone support, access to the huge online knowledgebase, guaranteed one hundred per cent network and infrastructure uptime and many other business-critical support features. To make this vision a reality, Rackspace has concentrated on three key areas to ensure that the fanatical support tradition endures: people, systems and processes.

Rackspace has done nothing particularly innovative. They took a commoditized technology service, targeted the key customer 'moments of truth' and focused their strategy, culture, people, systems and processes on ensuring that those are delivered 'fanatically' – in other words, they keep driving themselves to deliver for the customer. This has involved taking customer understanding seriously and creating what is, for them, a great service. This clearly illustrates that you do not necessarily need to develop the 'wow' customer experience or use highly sophisticated customer relationship systems, monitoring and measurement; you can do the simple things really well and achieve success.

Setting or changing your organization's customer service strategy, culture and policies is relatively easy to do as part of the project to implement or update. It is not easy to maintain the focus that organizations such as Rackspace have achieved. Once you've set your customer service strategy in motion, you need continually to do all – or most – of the things identified in this book. The best companies that differentiate their products based on service will last longer, be more profitable, and attract the loyalty of existing and new customers. The Harvard Service Profit Chain model shows an investment in internal service quality and service staff retention and productivity as ultimately delivering customer loyalty and profitability with increased revenues and profit (Heskett, Sasser and Schlesinger, 1997).

Breaking down the three elements in this chapter's title, strategy will very much drive policies, whereas culture is essentially created by you and the people across the business. To develop your strategy and policies, in this chapter I have already provided you with some guidance and examples. Philip Cullum, deputy chief executive of the National Consumer Council, now part of Consumer Direct, said in his 2006 report *The Stupid Company: How British Businesses Throw Away Money by Alienating Consumers*:

> 70 per cent of consumers tell us that company bosses are out of touch, with no idea what it's like to be a customer. Most people say they'd be happy to help companies improve if they thought anyone was listening, but that most of the time it's easier to simply walk away (though many then tell all their friends). The message is that as you grow bigger, you have to work harder to get it right. (Cullum, 2006)

This quote shows how difficult it can be to show to customers that you listen to them and build what they say into your strategy. But what business are you really in? Many organizations make the mistake, when putting a business strategy in place, of saying 'Our mission is customer service' or 'The customer is our business' or 'We exist to delight the customer'. That is not true – you are there to sell cars, computer systems, food, financial services, or whatever your core business is. Even if your services are not sold and you work in a public sector or charitable organization, your main mission is to produce and deliver your services. Customer service is just one of the important tools to accomplish that mission. For example, if your business is car sales, the best service in the world will not sell cars if you have neglected to order the stock to fill the showroom.

There are many potential examples of customer strategies to use as templates, and below I have used an extract from Aberdeenshire Council's strategy to illustrate how you might set out your customer service policies to support the overall business vision or mission:

> The customer feedback loop sits at the core of Aberdeenshire's customer service strategy. It involves the ongoing process of:
>
> - setting standards through customer service charter(s);
> - communicating these to the public;
> - capturing feedback through the customer feedback (complaints) scheme, residents surveys and other feedback;

- reviewing performance; and
- using the outcome of this review process to revise the customer service standards contained in the customer service charter.

(Aberdeenshire Customer Service Strategy, 2007)

To achieve the underlying strategy and policies is a reasonably simple task that blends the business and service aims together, telling people what you are aiming to achieve in your customer service model. You will remember I noted earlier that culture is essentially created by you and the people across your business. The Rackspace example is a clear illustration of a culture defined by the people-based, customer-oriented core values of the business. In my experience that is only achieved by the CEO or a senior management 'champion' setting in place and living these values. It is then only maintained by managers and employees across the business continually living and endorsing those values.

> **Case study 5: Zappos**
>
> Zappos is an online shoe business based in Las Vegas that Amazon bought for $850m in summer 2009. Zappos is renowned for providing world-class service, and the entire company is committed to succeed in that. The staff commits to show these values in their words and actions. They know it is not just up to the management to promote the culture – it is everybody's responsibility. Their ability to keep the 'small family' work ethic that they created in its early days and to maintain the core values as the company has grown has further reinforced their service reputation. The 10 Zappos core values are:
>
> - deliver wow through service;
> - be passionate and determined;
> - embrace and drive change;
> - build a positive team and family spirit;
> - do more with less;
> - pursue growth and learning;
> - create fun and a little weirdness;
> - build open and honest relationships with communication;
> - be adventurous, creative and open-minded;
> - be humble.
>
> (Sullivan and Siefker, 2009)

The culture at Rackspace and Zappos is both passionate and committed. Each culture is different and has been adapted to suit each organization, but they share similar values. These are constantly lived and revisited by managers with staff at all levels to ensure service is both consistent and improving. You can achieve the success that both Rackspace and Zappos have had in creating customer service led cultures by ensuring staff and managers are focusing on key service factors like measuring service quality and feedback from the customer every day, and using and reinforcing this at staff meetings. They should also explain why excellent customer service is important for the company, and what the company do that makes life easier for everyone. Make sure you communicate excellent examples of customer service both within and outside the company and celebrate them. Encourage everyone to have a sense of responsibility for group performance and help employees see how their performance affects others. If people really do not buy into these types of actions and messages, should they really be employed in customer service roles?

You will note the emphasis on communication, in particular when setting the expectations of customers, and when setting out the expected behaviours of staff members. Also worth noting is the advice to eliminate routines and processes that work against the customer. Although this might not always be entirely possible because of legislative requirements – for example when banks are required to confirm identity to carry out transactions even though you have held an account for 20 years – every effort *must* be made to make the process as simple and painless as possible. Staff, too, can be targeted for removal from their role if they are not suitable for a service role – all of us will have experienced poor service from people clearly not right for a customer-facing job.

This part of the chapter, as you may have noticed, is dominated by lists, and this will help you to form your own to establish your strategy, policies and culture from your consultation with the key customer stakeholders in your organization. If you are in any doubt as to the value of creating your list, consider the requirements included in the Singapore Airlines job description for cabin crew: 'Delivering excellent service to passengers is also an important aspect of being a cabin crew. Our Cabin Crew appreciate and are ever ready to address the special needs of each unique customer' (Singapore Airlines, 2009). This sums up why the airline is so successful and why it continually wins awards in this area.

This last example further reinforces the earlier lists of values from Zappos and Rackspace and underlines the fact that the decisions that you make on setting the strategy, policies and culture will help to enable your organization to keep up with, or ahead of, the leaders in your industry.

People – leadership, structure and management

People are the single most important element to enable you to deliver great customer service, and they should be very much in mind at the time of setting your strategic aims in place. Decisions should be based on the strategies and policies relating to the recruitment, development and retention of staff. This applies whether it is for your own organization, or if you have responsibility for a whole industry sector.

People 1st is the sector skills body for the hospitality industry. Brian Wisdom, chief executive of People 1st, believes the UK hospitality industry needs to 'raise the bar' in order to compete with other tourist destinations, especially in the run up to the London 2012 Olympic Games and Paralympic Games. Wisdom has stated that 'the customer service skills of frontline and supervisory staff are critical to the hospitality industry's success as their behaviour and actions impact on whether visitors have had an excellent or bad experience and are likely to return,' (caterersearch.com, 2009).

In order to get the best out of even the most skilled service staff, you will need to have in place the correct leadership and management and a staffing structure that reflects your desire to focus on providing great customer service. It is important to realize that leadership is not the same as management – good leaders often do not make good managers and vice versa. Perhaps one of the best-known business leaders today is Richard Branson of Virgin. He could confidently be described as having the vision and entrepreneurial flair to identify and exploit opportunities, but in order to turn those opportunities into successful businesses he appoints excellent managers to run them and to deliver the products or services. Leadership is typically longer term and visionary; management is shorter term and delivery- or task-oriented. Organizations wanting to deliver great service will not just need an inspirational service-oriented leader but will also need managers who can deliver the vision.

The structure of staffing for customer service-oriented businesses must always reflect the customer-led nature of the business. The business exists because customers want your products or services, so a staffing structure should always be designed with this in mind. Looking at it 'from the outside in' and establishing what you need to achieve for the customer is vital.

Processes and technology

Processes are essential for all sizes of organization, allowing good practice to be carried out again and again to a tried and trusted method, regardless of who carries it out.

BS 8477 offers guidance to customer service managers responsible for: 'maintaining the effective and efficient operation of the customer service process, including the recruitment and training of appropriate employees, technology requirements, documentation, setting and meeting target timelines and other requirements, and process reviews' and highlights areas such as complaints that require sound processes. A particular example that would be useful in tracking and tuning your service strategy would be 'reporting to top management on customer service outcomes, with recommendations for improvement'. This is contained in subclause 4.2 of the standard.

Current research indicates that customers are still experiencing high levels of poor service, and in '*Customers: Who Cares?*', a UK customer care survey from the Customer Care Alliance, November 2008, of the 10,102 consumers who took part, 78 per cent experienced at least one problem with the products and services they consumed during the last year, and only 10 per cent of consumers were completely satisfied with the way the organization handled their problem. The report goes on to say that 'there remains a worrying reluctance from UK organizations to provide ongoing customer care to existing customers when they need it' (Customer Care Alliance, 2008). Much of this can be attributed to the lack of sound processes, as often the 'first contact' of service is of an acceptable standard, otherwise we would not purchase the product or service in the first place.

So, processes that cover every stage of the service lifecycle will need to be developed, with a senior manager taking responsibility, and focusing particularly on making the customer contact area and follow-up as effective and streamlined as possible. BS 8477 recommends focusing on the following areas:

- timelines/responsiveness – for dealing with customer enquiries, processing customer orders, delivery, meeting appointment times, complaint handling;
- provision of information to customers – both before and after purchase;
- customer interaction – for accessibility, counter service, telephone service, online service, customer appointments for sales, service and repair.

Technology – which might be anything from a paper ledger recording customer complaints and incidents to a multimillion pound software system offering customer records, relationship management and knowledgebases – will generally enhance the way a process works. However, many organizations have previously made the error of selecting and buying an expensive piece of technology before really considering or establishing effective processes.

Technology can help to refine your thinking on how your processes can be developed. It is advantageous, especially in a new organization, to design processes alongside selecting your technology; technology will not, however, replace the fundamental need to plan, implement and document sound processes.

Processes and technology will take a large amount of project time to develop and select respectively. Processes will be heavily dependent on the person or people developing them and the technology selection will be dependent on the time-consuming processes of market research, short-listing and testing before a decision can be made.

Total quality management and continual service improvement

Great customer service delivered once – 'what does this customer, whom I'm dealing with right now, want?' – to a customer is good. But it is not good enough for the longer-term benefit to the organization as it might not guarantee customer loyalty. The incidence of good service has set a high level of expectation with the customer, meaning that they expect at least this level of service every other time they come into contact with the business. This is the continual competitive nature of most service arenas in today's world. For example, it is now accepted that your car will be washed and vacuumed when it is being serviced. This was unheard of 20 years ago, but is now expected – in fact we are likely to complain if it does *not* happen. In business class on most airlines there are 'flat-bed' seats to help you sleep on a long flight, and a simple large reclining seat is now considered insufficient. This is a major advance from 10 years ago.

When what was once considered 'a great customer experience' becomes a commonplace customer expectation, you need to keep that customer loyal to your organization by adopting a philosophy of continual service improvement, which will seek to add a little extra to 'beat' customer expectation at each return visit. Chris Daffy, in his book *Once a Customer, Always a Customer*, calls these his '+1s', and it could be as simple as the garage telling the customer 'we noticed your boot was a bit muddy so we've cleaned it for you' or 'there was a chip on your bonnet that we've touched in'.

Many of the customer service principles recommended by BS 8477 are directly related to this type of ongoing improvement and the areas around it, for example:

- identification of customer service issues – there should be systematic identification and management of customer service issues relevant to an organization's operations;
- customer service quality – the whole organization should be involved in the development and ongoing review of customer service quality, developed from a customer perspective, relevant to their area of operation;

- feedback systems – effective feedback systems for customers and employees should be developed and maintained;
- continual improvement – systems should be developed to ensure that the level of customer service is relevant to, or exceeds, current customer expectations.

This area is where customer service overlaps with total quality management (TQM), which had its roots in the quality improvement methods applied largely to the manufacture and development of products in the late 20th century. The Japanese and Americans were pre-eminent in the development of quality methodologies such as Kaizen, Six Sigma and TQM. These were particularly effective in helping to improve the quality of output from factories in the post-Second World War rebuilding of Japanese manufacturing and their subsequent development to become the dominant motor vehicle and electronic supplier of the age, especially in terms of product quality. Put into simple terms, these methodologies were intended to achieve both a consistent level of product quality and to encourage ongoing improvement in that product quality or effectiveness.

In Europe, similar methodologies were applied from the European Foundation for Quality Management (EFQM) and the BS ISO 9001 quality standard, which at one stage was so dominant that many organizations refused to buy products from companies without that certification. The EFQM model is shown here:

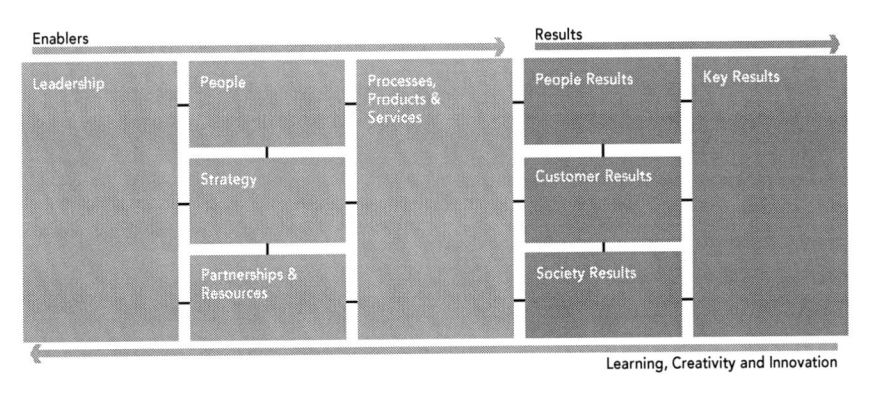

Figure 6. EFQM excellence model (2009) – http://ww1.efqm.org/en/Home/aboutEFQM/Ourmodels/TheEFQMExcellenceModel/tabid/170/Default.aspx.

How this applies to customer service today is evident from the inclusion of many 'quality principles' in customer service operations. One that works especially well is derived from the Kaizen quality principle where each week or month you identify the top 10 defect areas and seek to eliminate them to improve the product quality.

The same principle when applied to the top 10 customer service incident areas will have an effect of ongoing customer service improvement by eliminating the most common customer problems. It will also highlight any root causes of such incidents that may relate to a product quality or operational process problem that can then also be corrected. Indeed, after a major failure that has affected customer service – such as the loss of the computer system that provides a bank's ATM network – some organizations use a 'major incident post-mortem' analysis to learn from the incident and to prevent such incidents reoccurring.

A good example of exactly this type of service quality improvement programme has been implemented recently at the Shop Direct Group, which includes the Littlewoods, Great Universal, and Kays home and online shopping brands. Their 'Customer 1st Aid' programme highlights both customer issues (such as poor shopping experiences) and business failures. The subsequent resolution of these types of incident has led to both an improvement in customer service and higher levels of efficiency, delivering an estimated £3.1m saving to the group. The changes made to the home delivery service alone have saved £124,000 and reduced the number of customer incidents logged by 50 per cent (Wall, 2009).

Ideas, innovation and refinement

So, customer service can be improved by the application of tried and tested quality improvement methods. Not surprisingly, especially in well-established larger organizations, there are some excellent systems and methods in place to do that. Where such organizations often fail is in improving service with new ideas and innovation. That is not necessarily because nobody in the organization has ideas or suggestions that lead to service innovation and improvement, but often that these are not captured and applied.

first direct, the internet and telephone bank, has already been highlighted in Chapter 2 as a brand with a reputation for great service. To add to its credentials, and to reward customers who opted to take their bank statements online rather than on paper, first direct committed to and carried out a planting programme of both virtual and real trees. It has also launched a 'Little Black Book', which is effectively a social networking site for the bank's customers that also offers interesting things to do and places to go. The bank justifies these initiatives with its often used line 'nothing to do with banking, but everything to do with first direct'. To the bank's customers, they are small but innovative additions to the services that it sees from the bank. To the bank, they are very much part of an ongoing programme to innovate continually and to refresh its offer to customers and keep them loyal.

Marks & Spencer has spent significant sums on Mary Gober's customer service training, putting every Marks & Spencer employee in the UK through a structured workshop on the tools and skills required to provide great customer service. This is believed to have boosted sales and reduced staff turnover in the recovery of the business over the last few years. This is just one example of a brand that is well respected for the service it offers needing to invest in the refinement of that offer to keep it fresh.

The staff suggestion scheme has often been the official route for ideas, but unless staff members are actively encouraged as part of their job to think of new ways to improve service – *and* they get feedback on its submission, evaluation and acceptance or rejection, and/or reward and recognition for its implementation if accepted – they will quickly lose interest in the scheme.

> A PricewaterhouseCoopers innovation study conducted in 2000 claimed 29% of viable ideas come from employees, while 46% come from customers, suppliers and market intelligence. It found a 'structured idea management process' – gathering ideas from staff, customers and suppliers – was a major innovation success factor.
>
> [Steve Procter, operations director of ideasUK] says ideasUK asks its 160 members every year how much money they save by implementing ideas generated by staff suggestion schemes. 'Each year [results show] savings of between £80m to £90m from staff ideas,' he says. (Charlton, 2009).

The continual 'supply of ideas and innovation' can be significantly enhanced by the existence of a culture such as those previously mentioned at Rackspace and Zappos. If managers and staff are continually 'living the values', they will be seeking to improve the service to customers and the processes and products as part of their everyday role. Nigel Barlow's book, *Re-think: How to think differently*, lists seven areas where 're-thinking' your current beliefs and mindset can throw up opportunities for improvements in what you do both in life and in business:

- Spring clean your beliefs.
- Buy a new newspaper.
- Approach today with 'open page thinking'.
- Be a creator, not a critic.
- Pay attention.
- Teach yourself ignorance.
- Rediscover family rituals.

(Barlow, 2006)

Barlow's main points stem from the fact that we all develop views and opinions that can become entrenched over time and potentially limit our ability to think afresh about a familiar area at work or at home or leisure. Applying his list – by gaining new perspectives from reading a different newspaper, looking at your job as if you had just started today, listening more carefully to everything that people are telling us, or not greeting every new suggestion with 'I hear what you say, but' – offers us the chance to revisit our opinions and perhaps look at situations relating to customers with fresh eyes.

Ideas and innovation are the lifeblood of future customer service enhancements and are vital to increase the loyalty of customers. Disney's theme parks are an excellent case in point. They identified several years ago that queuing for the most popular rides was a huge source of customer frustration, so they introduced entertainment for the waiting queues from specialist 'queue entertainers'. Alongside this they marked points in the queue 'One hour from here, 30 minutes from here' and then made sure the customer took less time than that to get to the ride. This is an excellent example of turning a potentially negative customer experience into one where customer expectation is exceeded. Other theme parks followed Disney's lead, and this then led to the introduction of the 'priority pass', where customers can jump to the front of the queue on some rides by pre-purchasing a limited number of tickets to bypass the main queue.

These types of idea are part of the continual drive to improve the customer's perception of your service, often by focusing on some of the areas that are not necessarily 'part of the product itself'. Queues are certainly not part of Disney's product, but have been turned into an area of competitive advantage. Similarly, easyJet now offers 'speedy boarding' on their flights for a small fee, giving the customer the option to bypass the boarding queue and get first choice of seats by being among the first to board. Ryanair operates a similar system.

These are simple examples of how innovation in one industry can be adapted to improve service offerings in another industry. It is your responsibility continually to keep abreast of what is happening in other organizations – and then to see whether there is a way that you can improve your offering by adapting what they are doing. For easyJet and Ryanair it also represents another revenue-generating opportunity: they have addressed an area of customer frustration that they generated by their own business model through not allocating seat numbers at check-in and turned it into an area of revenue-earning advantage. This illustrates the power of such innovation and the generation and capture of ideas.

Customer retention and loyalty

It is essential to keep your customers loyal. For example, the leading consulting firm, Bain & Co, quoted in the report *The Positive Economics of Customer Engagement* from Allegiance, LaMalfa, K. (2007), has estimated that a 5 per cent increase in customer retention can lead to a 75 per cent increase in profitability. Further data from the report confirm that British businesses and organizations should recognize that a greater and genuine focus on retaining existing customers can be a more effective business strategy than continual acquisition. Loyal customers not only continue to buy products and services, but also generate powerful advertising by giving recommendations to friends and relatives.

Seventy-eight per cent of the consumers surveyed for the Institute of Customer Service report in 2008 experienced at least one problem with products or services used during the last year; the most common problems were that the product or service did not meet expectations (37 per cent); poor product or service quality (30 per cent); and unsatisfactory service (unrelated to repair) (26 per cent). Eighty-three per cent with a serious problem contacted or complained to the organization responsible and 45 per cent shared the experience with friends or colleagues – on average 10 people were told of a negative experience.

All of this data suggests that the focus on keeping customers satisfied – often by simply meeting expectations of the product or service – will both retain them and reduce the chance of them effectively working against your organization by telling potential customers what a bad experience they had with you. This is further reinforced by the Strativity research below, which suggests that customers who are 'promoters' will do business with the organization for a longer period:

Despite the amount of research in this area, which supports the suggestion that loyal customers are a good thing, it will probably never be entirely *proved*, as customers leave for all sorts of reasons, such as moving house or changing jobs. However, common sense indicates that attracting new customers and keeping your existing ones is better than continually losing customers and needing to replace them.

At the 2008 Loyalty Expo, John Dawson of DataCo spoke about attrition (customers leaving) and keeping current customers (Payton, 2009). He focused on the importance of studying your company's demographics. What are your customers doing? When and why are they leaving? What can you do to prevent further attrition? His experience mirrored mine in that sometimes the reasons for attrition are simple: customer service is not up to par; prices are not competitive and service is not good quality. These are things that are quite easy to fix.

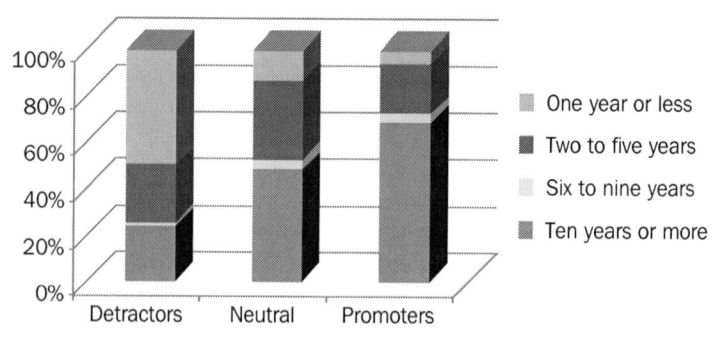

If the experience I receive remains constant, I expect to continue to do business with this business for another:

- One year or less
- Two to five years
- Six to nine years
- Ten years or more

Figure 7. Strativity Group 2009 Customer Experience Consumer Study: consumers pay for exceptional customer experiences.

What about loyalty to the company's brand? Are your clients ready to stick with you no matter what? Do you give them a reason to? Dawson said that while, in his experience, most marketing budgets dedicate only about 20 per cent to customer retention, it should be closer to 50 per cent. He recommends these steps to keep a customer loyal to your brand:

- Drive engagement – encourage customers to want to be a part of your brand.
- Watch for continued relevance – do not assume that what you started doing to get your customers' attention will work for ever.
- Maintain quality and frequency of communication – if you send emails or direct mail, give your customers a reason to want to read it. And do not bombard them with mail.
- Liven up your programme – add new offers, new rewards and new business partners to keep your customers excited.

(Payton, 2009)

Customers are too valuable to lose, especially when you can do something to retain them.

Customer satisfaction measurement and feedback

In this book we have established that we need to understand our customers, keep them satisfied, give them a great experience and keep them coming back. Without some sort of measurement process that captures our performance level against set targets (covered in more detail in Chapter 7), feedback from customers on how they think we are doing and some trend history that tracks whether we're getting better or worse, how do we know if we're succeeding or failing?

Below are four simple indicators that will help you to determine whether your organization is succeeding or failing:

- You're still in business where some competitors are not.
- Your sales levels are competitive in your marketplace.
- You regularly see returning customers and attract customers by the recommendation of others.
- People seem to like your organization and talk about you in good terms, often thanking you for the things you do for them.

These indicators are not always measurable and often can be judged only by their 'feel', but I have always found them to be utterly reliable. While developing your success or failure indicators you will need to work out what success is for your organization. The indicators above will be fairly useless, for example, if success is to get into the market with a great product that everyone wants, make millions of pounds profit in a short timeframe and then get out before the competition catches up.

To develop meaningful business-oriented measures, you therefore have to start with defining what success is for you, i.e. defining a target range of indicators. If you consider the question 'what level of service is it that your organization wants – or needs – to achieve?' you need to set your indicators as to how you will gauge your performance against this level of service. Then you need to consider the way in which you will measure and report them. Lastly, what are the ways you will use to ask for, capture and apply the feedback of your customers?

Whatever questions you might develop to ask your customers, and whatever complaints management process you have set up to manage things when you do not get it right, these two key questions will give you much of what you need to know:

- What do we do well, or that you like, that you want us to do more of?
- What do we do badly, or that you do not like, that you would like us to stop or do less of?

All of these areas will be covered in more detail in Chapter 7, but they are key issues you should think about during your planning phase.

Summary

Where do we start?

This is a common cry from organizations looking to establish consistently great service for their customers. Building the attributes of reputation, performance, growth, profitability and trust (as suggested in the Institute of Customer Service model at the start of this chapter) into a customer service model that fits your unique mix of people, products and services takes time, and the areas of focus recommended in this chapter require a huge amount of commitment and persistence to achieve.

Developing a sound business model for service that is appropriate for your organization and customers, and which is flexible and resilient, is, in my view, the only place to start. Many of the focus areas are pure common sense, but how many of us are still receiving poor service from organizations where common sense seems to have been abandoned? By building a model that works for you using a sound project plan, input from standards and other organizations, establishing what values and policies to adopt, ensuring you have reliable processes and technology, and having a culture that will include ideas and innovation, you will have your own lasting strategic approach for delivering great customer service.

The Institute of Customer Service *World-Class Customer Service* report provides an excellent closing example list of key differentiating factors for service delivery: listen to customers; analyse root causes of problems; segment customers based on different needs; train, engage and recruit great people; continually improve and reduce errors; innovate; use IT as an enabler; encourage an accountable, consistent service delivery; have a clear strategy and leadership; brand recognition; be connected and trustworthy with proactive communications (Johns, 2008).

You should certainly develop a clear service ethos, such as those of Rackspace or Zappos. You might not have a charismatic leader like Richard Branson to call on to create your brand image, but you will be able to create your own service brand strategy and policies. This will form a base for you to grow a service-led culture that will help to maintain it. That maintenance is absolutely essential and requires ongoing tactical and strategic evaluation and possible retuning.

Learning points

In this chapter we have focused on how to build your own model to deliver great customer service to your customers and highlighted the principal areas you need to pay attention to in order to succeed.

The most important points to remember are listed below:

- Understand, before you start, what level of service it is that your organization wants – or needs – to achieve. Remember that you are not in the customer service business: you sell cars, groceries, provide public services. You use customer service as a way to help to sell and to service whatever your primary revenue generators are.
- Understand what your competitors, other comparable businesses and businesses you admire are doing. Think about what you can adapt to fit your model.
- Use existing standards and models such as BS 8477 and those from the Institute of Customer Service to guide your thinking and planning. Perhaps you can employ a customer service 'steering group' as a sounding board.
- Use a project plan, or if you are a small organization, devise a list of the tasks that you need to accomplish so that you can track your progress.
- Understand how the quality industry can help you to improve your quality of service continually by applying quality management techniques to your processes and measurements. Ensure you know whether you are retaining customers and whether others are being recommended to you.
- Encourage ideas and innovation to keep developing and enhancing your products and services, in however small or large a way – from you, your staff and your customers. You can also look outside your industry for inspiration.
- Develop measures that give you continual feedback on how you might improve your customer service model.

The following is a short list of techniques and examples to consider and learn from.

Techniques to help develop your customer service model:

- Always ask tough questions of yourself/managers/directors/the steering group when developing your model, such as why do customers leave, or stay with you? Do we want to give different customers different levels of service? Who are our most profitable customers and what are they worth to us over their 'lifetime with us'? Dig deep early to allow you to design a model that really suits your organization.

- Apply your own learning. You will have had many service experiences yourself that will have taught you what you consider to be good service. On a recent holiday in a privately owned apartment in Croatia, the owner delivered warm doughnuts to us one morning – it might not seem much, but it was one of those small '+1s' that Chris Daffy referred to in his book. It made us think very positively about recommending the apartment to friends.
- Use your own 'pyramid of service', especially if you want to implement different levels of service for different customers.
- Adapt a list and use it as a guide, especially in terms of the communication elements of your plan. This will be particularly valuable to gain buy-in to your strategy.
- The quality improvement techniques such as the top 10 customer issues or the 'major incident post-mortem' are tried and tested techniques that will make service quality improvement easier. Make sure you use them.

Examples:

- The first direct 'Little Black Book' is an excellent example of a well-known service brand adding something extra to help keep customers interested. What is the equivalent in your business that you can add?
- Improving product and service quality through looking at industries outside your own can be an excellent way of improving your offer – Southwest Airlines, a US budget carrier, examined the pit-stop performance of a Formula One racing team to help them reduce the time it takes them to turn around aircraft at airports. They may seem to be worlds apart, but mechanical checks, pilot and crew co-ordination and fuelling are relevant to both.
- In the recession of 2008–9, many airlines chose to reduce costs by cutting out some of the 'frills' in their service, such as hot towels and free beverages. Although certainly understandable, in the long term it will be remembered by customers who may choose to fly with the airlines that continued to provide the 'frills'.
- In the catering sector, some restaurants that offered 50 per cent off in some of the online restaurant guides reduced their portions and quality of ingredients. This is counter-productive as the aim of the offer is to draw customers in and keep them coming back, so they should surely be offered the 'full portion service'.

4
Customer service people

The basics

Whatever you do with, to or for customers – whether your business is 100 per cent online or completely face to face – it is only possible with some form of human contact, or by you making an analysis of electronic transaction methods and adding a human 'feel' to them. All customers are looking for that 'human touch', whatever means you use to deal with them.

Amazon, for example, generally conducts all of its customer service electronically, but it has a well-known reputation for great service. That reputation is achieved by ensuring that your experience with them as a customer makes you feel 'looked after' and valued. The marketplace site eBay has a rating system for all its participants so that you can place trust in the buyers or sellers you interact with. Both of these organizations are 'self-service', usually with no direct employee contact, but work hard to give customers a human feel to their experience. So, even if your organization is never going to have face-to-face contact with a customer, the people you have are, of course, crucial to the quality of the service you deliver.

Customer service people are extremely important, and I am sure every director in every organization would support that. After all, many business mission statements tell us 'our people are our most important asset' or something similar. However, if that is the case, why are we still so often disappointed with the level of service we receive from some of the people we encounter in organizations? We have already highlighted survey results and quotes that show customers do not receive a consistent level of service, and this is often a result of a poor experience with an individual.

The answer is that although every organization tells you that it (customer service) is important, not every organization is committed to making sure their people are consistently great at service, and even if they are, then there will inevitably be occasional lapses. The occasional lapse is of course okay, and as a customer we would probably forgive it. No doubt the organization would be keen to use it as a learning point to improve further. Lack of commitment is not forgivable. The result can often be the different perception of a 'disconnected' management and that of a dissatisfied customer as evidenced below:

Contrasting views between CEOs and Customers

	Percent (%)
CEOs – we provide 'above average' customer service	~74
Customers – I was 'somewhat' to 'extremely' dissatisfied with my most recent customer service experience	~57

Accenture, 2007

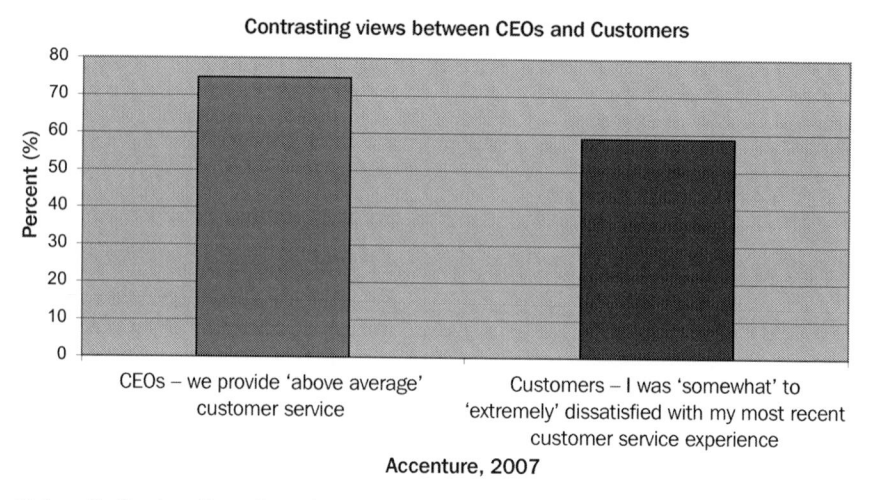

Figure 8: Contrasting views between CEOs and customers (Accenture, 2007).

An Institute of Customer Service research report, Customer *Priorities: What Customers Really Want*, identified a top 10 list of priorities: 'Overall quality of the product or service supplied; Friendliness of staff; Handling problems and complaints; Speed of service; Helpfulness of staff; Handling enquiries; Being treated as a valued customer; Competence of staff; Ease of doing business; Being kept informed' (Hill and Hampshire, 2006). The majority of these priorities are directly attributable to interaction with people. The Avis example from Chapter 1, in which staff members were trained to understand different customer cultural attitudes, was people oriented, and Jane's good heel bar experience from the same chapter was very much down to her experience with the staff.

It was mentioned earlier that a great product can be destroyed by a rude employee, and a commoditized product can be made great by an employee going beyond the call of duty in pursuit of delivering great customer service, making the customer experience more personal, more positive and more memorable. An Accenture report, *Leadership in Customer Service: Delivering on the Promise*, highlighted the public sector, where their products are often core elements of people's lives, such as housing and school services (Accenture, 2007). The conclusion was that 'future public service employees need to be customer service experts rather than paper processors or even subject matter experts. Otherwise, governments risk alienating the citizens who have to come through the high-touch channels because their needs are more intense' (Accenture, 2007). The report findings also showed that 64 per cent of citizens favoured telephone or 'walk-in' contact, further highlighting the importance of hiring and investing in the right people (Accenture, 2007).

I believe that you had enough justification to focus on your people before you got to this point in the book, but it is so important that I do not feel it is overkill to reinforce it here. This chapter will go on to highlight all of the important areas you need to focus on to help ensure that your organization has all of the people issues covered to build into your customer service model.

As in Chapter 3, it is possible to find good guidance in standards to outline the important people areas to focus on. For example, in BS 8477, the customer service obligations of various levels of managers and staff are outlined, and there is a practical annex with guidance on required staff competences, recruitment and training. These competences should include 'good interpersonal skills, including the ability to empathize with the customer; effective communication skills; handling stress; listening actively; working as part of a team; problem solving and complaints handling; a thorough knowledge of the organization's products and structure or the capacity to quickly acquire this knowledge; and commitment to the company's mission and values'.

In the Cabinet Office *Customer Service Excellence Standard* there is a set of criteria relating to the culture of the organization and how it should relate to the customer. This standard covers the leadership, policies and cultural aspects that we have raised already but also guidance on where to apply them, such as service planning, job descriptions and the recruitment process. The Service Desk Institute (SDI) Professional Standards give comprehensive guidance on the skills, attributes and behaviours required from service staff at all levels. The SDI Service Desk Foundation Standard gives a definitive list of the desired characteristics of a customer-facing service agent:

> Taking ownership of the customer's incident or request and seeing it through to resolution; conveying a sincere willingness to help; maintaining a positive attitude; treating all customers with respect and courtesy; focusing attention on the customer and on business needs while providing best possible service; setting customer expectations; creating a positive impression of the Service Desk; helping gain the customer's confidence and trust; building rapport and encouraging customers to return; listening and conveying empathy; working together and supporting the rest of the team; sharing ideas and innovations; taking responsibility and accountability for actions.

This list, although not complete or definitive for your specific organization, can be used as a starting point for selecting people for your customer service roles. For another example, Mary Gober identified a similar list in her 2003 book *The Art of Giving Quality Service* that her 'service-giver' (the generic name she used for anyone in a service role) had to have the right attitude towards customers, identifying the following qualities: enjoying helping people; handling people well; caring for their customers; giving fair and equal treatment to all and never using their job authority to 'punish' people (Gober, 2003). Mary goes on to add skills and qualities in other areas with particular emphasis on key communication and relationship skills (Gober, 2003).

Selecting and recruiting the right people

Despite the apparent commitment to their people, most companies do not spend enough time and effort preparing for the selection and recruitment of the right people. Hence each time you recruit, you enter a lottery and are lucky if the odds work in your favour and you recruit the staff you need who will be exactly right for a customer service role. Preparation can improve those odds – in particular by:

- establishing what personal strengths, attributes and behaviours you seek;
- developing a list of the skills you want in the recruit;
- using a range of tools and methods, however simple, to select candidates consistently for interview and possible recruitment.

BS 8477 states that 'a variety of recruitment techniques should be used that will reveal candidates that will fit the customer service oriented employee profile, and communicate job expectations as they relate to the organization's service mission'. Although interviews are an essential part of the recruitment process, many of us have had experiences where people who have interviewed well have not performed as we would want, so it is incredibly important to add some extra dimensions to the recruitment process to limit the chance of getting it wrong. Rudimentary, of course, is to create a list of the skills, behaviours and attitudes that you require from your new hire. You could include, for example, psychometric testing, telephone interview screening, role-playing, group tests or exercises and talent assessments.

There are many methods available to help you to select these qualities in your prospective staff, some of which have already been outlined. Caliper, which helps organizations to select their people via psychometric and other forms of testing, worked with the Institute of Customer Service to identify the traits exhibited by top performers in customer service roles. These traits are:

- problem solving – the ability to recognize abstract concepts and detect relationships in data;
- assertiveness – the degree of positive forcefulness an individual will use to control a situation;
- helpfulness – the willingness to be accommodating;
- confidence – the ability of a person to bounce back from rejection;
- thoroughness – the degree of perseverance and attention to detail;
- empathy – the ability to sense and respond accurately to the reactions of another person; and
- sociability – the ability and desire to be with and to work with other people.

Figure 9 shows the spread of the traits identified in the study.

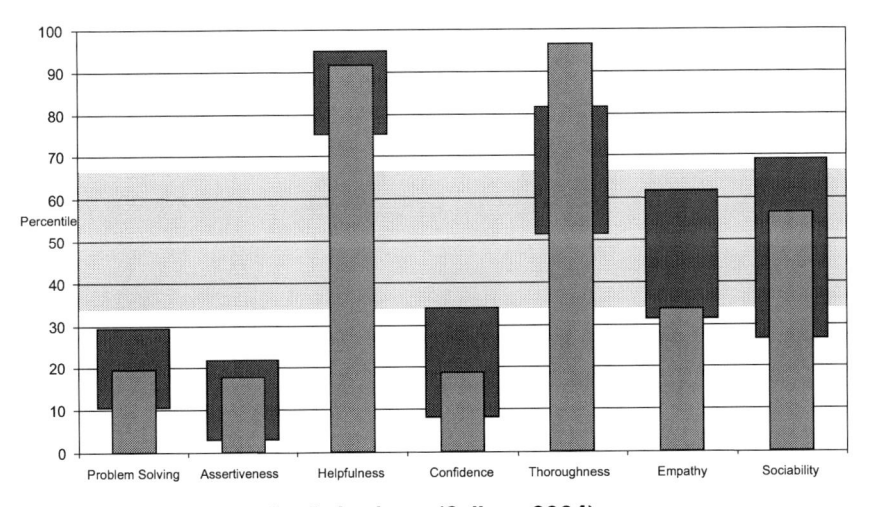

Figure 9. Customer service behaviours (Caliper, 2004).

The darker boxes show the commonality of the top performers; the smaller the box, the greater the similarity between such individuals. The vertical bars provide an example of how an individual might score on such a graph. The report went on to say:

> At that time, as now, there was much debate about whether customer service oriented personnel could be trained to also sell to their customers. The

concern was that even if this was possible for some customer service agents, there would be some compromise in overall customer service. Therefore, Caliper also assessed the results for the additional trait of ego-drive, or motivation to obtain a 'yes' from others.

In 2006 Caliper UK and the Institute of Customer Service collaborated again on another benchmark study, this time to ascertain the behavioural characteristics of face-to-face customer service representatives. There was an opinion that individuals who deal with their customers face to face would show very different personality characteristics and behaviours. The results in fact showed that the core qualities of top performers across all seven traits were much the same. The hypothesis is that those who have to deal directly face to face with their customers rather than over the phone (which perhaps could feel more 'anonymous') may tend to feel a greater sense of responsibility to that customer to follow through with commitments that they make (Caliper UK and Institute of Customer Service, 2006).

To confirm the importance of the contribution of people, Accenture's report, *High-Performance Workforce Study* (2002/2003) recorded that 74 per cent of executives believed that people issues are somewhat or significantly more important to their company's success than they were in the previous year. Reinforcing this notion is the fact that four of the five most important strategic priorities identified by executives are workforce related:

- attracting and retaining skilled staff;
- increasing customer care and service;
- improving workforce performance;
- changing leadership and management behaviours;
- changing organizational culture and employee attitudes.

(Accenture, 2002/2003)

However, survey participants also noted that there were shortcomings in their workforce that compromised their ability to compete effectively. Just 27 per cent of respondents said that the vast majority of their employees (over 75 per cent of their overall workforce) had the skills necessary to execute their jobs at an industry-leading level; only 12 per cent of respondents reported that more than 75 per cent of their workforce fully understood the company's strategic priorities; and just 17 per cent said more than 75 per cent of their employees understand the connection between their jobs and corporate strategy execution (Accenture, 2002/2003).

Correspondingly, unless you go through the exercise of deciding the mix of skills and attributes that you need it will be much more difficult to recruit the right people. Having established who you want, and having decided on the likely recruitment, evaluation and assessment processes, where do you find these people? Although some of it can be put down to sheer good luck, finding the right people means working hard to find the right source and route to hire the staff you want. Some organizations successfully advertise and recruit staff from within; some have a policy of hiring only graduate-level staff; some swear by a long-standing recruitment agency relationship; and others use web-based recruitment sites as a favoured path. There are many customer service managers who have a strategy of trying to recruit anyone they meet who impresses them with good service and attitude – seeing someone 'in action' who is unaware they are being assessed for recruitment can be a good alternative to a staged role play.

Having committed all this effort and expenditure to recruit your people, you now have to use them effectively, and although it would be simple to assume that people come with a built-in gene that makes them work hard, in the way that you want, for a fair remuneration, life often does not work that smoothly. We established in Chapter 3 that there were several elements that contributed to creating the right customer service model, and there are potentially as many to get your people working as you want them to.

Leadership and management

Once you have got the right people, how do you get them working how you want them to? Mostly, it comes down to how you apply the following six concepts: culture, motivation, emotion, passion, leadership and management. There are four main ways in which you can best apply these concepts to your staff, whether they number one, 10 or 1,000 or more.

> *Culture.* Set in place the culture you want to form a backdrop and ethos for your organization. The examples in Chapter 3 from Rackspace and Zappos offer guidance on the values that you could adopt, but I would urge you to develop your own to reflect the personality you want your business to achieve.
>
> *Leadership.* If you are a charismatic leader or entrepreneur like Richard Branson, then use that charisma for all it is worth to champion the culture and values you want to set and perpetuate. If that person does not exist in your organization, then you will need to step up to champion the values and convince the CEO to support them, consistently.

Management. Managers in your organization, in addition to doing their job, need to live, encourage and reinforce the values every day.

Motivation, emotion and passion. These words sum up why we bother to do anything. If you cannot turn on the motivational switch, or ignite the emotion or passion that exists within every member of staff, then the odds are that you will never deliver consistently great service.

Forrester senior analyst Bruce Temkin's insight on the key role of CEOs in *Customer Experience Matters* supports the leadership point when he says 'the focus on customer experience must come from the CEO's clear belief that it impacts business results. It is a core business imperative, not a "nice to have" initiative'. He goes on to emphasize the ongoing requirement to stay involved: 'This effort requires the active involvement and commitment by the CEO because transformation efforts can easily get bogged down in politics and silos. So reviewing progress of the firm's customer experience efforts needs to become a regular part of the executive agenda' (Temkin, 2009).

Turning on the motivational switch and igniting the passions and emotions of your people is one of the most written about areas, and not just in business. It applies, for example, in sport and music, where a team manager or conductor may be responsible for bringing together a team of talented and possibly highly paid individual players or musicians to deliver a winning performance in a match or concert. Although the sector is different, the principle is the same – bringing together individuals with individual strengths, talents and skills to form a good team that works towards a common goal or goals. In both cases they will spend many days, weeks and months establishing how the individual strengths of each player or musician can be moulded into the team or orchestra so that the best possible team can be developed. The team may suffer the injury or transfer of some of its members, but if the work has been put in to build a cohesive team with the above four points addressed, it will still be able to deliver a good performance.

The parallels are so powerful in different sectors that many successful leaders forge a living by telling others about how they have built and developed successful teams. As an example, the world-famous conductor, Benjamin Zander, uses the metaphor of the orchestra and a lifetime of experience conducting, coaching and teaching musicians to work his magic to overcome barriers to corporate productivity.

One of the world's most successful football teams, Manchester United, has won the English League title eleven times under manager, Sir Alex Ferguson. Although the team has clearly changed over the years, it has consistently delivered success. Even in the years when it has not won the title, it has usually been in the top three or four teams. Sir Alex is well known for his ability to instil pride in his players for the Manchester United 'brand', and also for his ability to merge locally developed youth talent with experienced 'stars' bought from other teams. These abilities have forged a 'winner's culture' at the club and an impressive winning record for the team.

It is likely that you do not have a sports team or orchestra to manage, but it is still possible to turn your team into winners. It is, as illustrated above, very much about establishing your overall goal and values, and then identifying the individual strengths of people in your team so that you can harness them to best effect in conjunction with those of the other team members. In the same way that a football team has strikers to score goals using attacking strategies and tactics, and defenders to prevent goals, you have people suited to different roles in carrying out team tasks using processes and procedures to meet organizational goals and the delivery of service to customers.

Buckingham and Clifton (2001) in *Now, Discover your Strengths* identified how a Gallup poll had asked 198,000 employees in 36 organizations 'at work do you have the opportunity to do what you do best every day?' The results showed that only 20 per cent felt that their strengths were in play every day. More disturbingly, it emerged that as people climbed the career ladder within their organization, they tended to do what they were good at even less. Buckingham and Clifton go on to explain how you can identify your strengths, with the reasoning that if you do not know your own strengths and the strengths of the people you are managing, then you could be in the wrong job, and as a manager or leader, be unable to get the best from your team.

That makes sense, and one of the ways in which you might know what you are good at and enjoy doing is to find activities that make you ask, 'When can I do this again?' Other signs, such as 'spontaneous reactions, yearnings, rapid learning and satisfaction will all help you detect the traces of your talents' (Buckingham and Clifton, 2008). This will also, of course, influence who you recruit, as you will be looking for strengths, skills and attributes that fit your values and complement the other members of your team.

So if you can identify both your and your team's strengths that is a great start, but what if you are still not sure about what the difference is between leading and managing the team, and therefore what role you should play? David Taylor (2002), formerly a corporate IT director, is now a top leadership speaker and consultant and in his book *The Naked Leader* (2002) states that 'a leader inspires loyalty based on who they are, and on what they do, not because of their job title'. He goes on to identify some ways to help the bonding process with the culture and with you as the leader:

- Encourage open, blame-free debate in your team, draw out everyone's contributions, hopes, fears and ideas for the future.
- Be a visible leader and talk/listen to people – and make sure you know their names off by heart.
- Consult widely and put in place a set of values everyone can identify with – and include fun or happiness as one of them.
- Catch people doing something right and openly thank or praise them – and you take responsibility for everything that goes wrong.

(Taylor, 2002)

So whether or not your title incorporates the words manager or leader, you should act as the latter. Taylor's list is simple for you to adopt and can apply in any sector, as it largely focuses on developing your communication skills and understanding the people you work with.

After you have established the strengths, the trust and the loyalty of your team, it is much easier to work on appealing to their emotions and passions to motivate them to deliver great service to their customers – consistently. At the SDI in 2003 we ran a workshop with Di Kamp, the CEO of Meta, a company that helps to develop teams and their managers. The group of customer service directors and managers was asked to develop their own list of ideas to motivate their teams. After an hour of individual and group discussion they suggested the following ideas:

- Devise five things you can do to make a difference to your own motivation – and another five for the people around you.
- People value feedback and self-development opportunities – use 360 degree, one-to-one meetings, which are excellent in providing the opportunity.
- Work smarter to create more time for you and your people, for example making better use of meeting time and scheduling email slots during the day to minimize interruptions.
- Work out what motivates you and you might get close to understanding what works to motivate others too.
- Get your people active and positive.
- Create the framework for a 'grown-up' environment.
- Be a leader: it is up to you to set values and a clear direction.
- Communicate the message clearly and often.
- Make your workplace a good place to be – fun and flexible.
- Make everyone feel 'part of it' – valued and trusted.
- Introduce where possible experienced mentors/angels for newer staff.

These customer service leaders were able to come up with a great list that they could draw on to make their workplaces better for their team and thereby increase motivation. One recent global success story, Google, has developed its own unique corporate culture – as shown in case study 6.

> **Case study 6: Google**
>
> Although Google has grown a lot since it opened in 1998, it tries to keep a small company feel. …if you visit their website they highlight features of Google culture at length – everyone eats in the office café, sitting with 'Googlers' from any of the different teams in that location. They encourage sharing ideas and opinions, believing that each 'Googler' is an equally important part to their success. Larry and Sergey [Google founders] ask for questions in weekly 'all-hands' meetings.
>
> Their corporate headquarters, nicknamed the 'Googleplex' in California, is one of many offices around the globe, and they all tend to share some essential elements. For example they cite 'Local expressions of each location, from a mural in Buenos Aires to ski gondolas in Zurich…bicycles or scooters for efficient travel between meetings…'Googlers' sharing cubes, yurts and huddle rooms – and very few solo offices.'

Google has taken just 10 years to dominate the internet search engine market, so the clearly relaxed environment would seem to both attract and motivate the type of staff it wants. The chapter to date has highlighted the importance of such shared values, the link between your own and your team's motivation, and the benefit of clear goals and direction.

One factor that is implicit in both Di Kamp's workshop and the Google case study is the importance of 'fun', which I believe is an essential facet of work today. If you do not enjoy at least some of your day at work then unless you were born into a wealthy family or get very lucky on the lottery, around one third of your life will not be as fulfilling as it could be.

Most people do not equate their working life with having fun. In some of the austere factory and office environments that existed in the early and in some cases late part of the 20th century, most managers discouraged having fun at work. You were there to work and the only fun you were allowed was with your workmates in your lunch and tea breaks. As a society, we, in the 21st century, believe it is a positive thing to enjoy your job. Managers encourage staff to have fun when they are at work, while still getting the job done. Some managers are not good at or comfortable with promoting fun, so if that is the case with your team, find someone in the team who can help.

If you need further inspiration, however, there are some great motivational books you can use to help. The best books I have come across to help inject the fun and inspiration into a customer service workplace are almost always short – an example is *The Buzz: 50 Little Things That Make a Big Difference to Serve Your Customer* by David Freemantle (2004), in which he highlights '50 little things' that will help staff to improve service. One such idea is to 'challenge yourself every day', which suggests small customer relationship enhancing activities such as personalizing a customer interaction. *Polar Bear Pirates* by Adrian Webster uses cartoon characters to illustrate ways to overcome negative characteristics to create a good team working culture. Sheldon Bowles' and Ken Blanchard's *Raving Fans* is a simple customer service improvement story from the author who wrote *One-Minute Manager*. It tells the story of a new area manager who needs to raise service standards, taking him on a journey of discovery through simple motivational techniques such as giving regular feedback to staff, telling them if they are doing well or need to improve, and how best staff can work with customers to add value to the customer experience.

So, even if there is no one in your team to take on the role of 'motivator', there is plenty of help available in a very cost-effective range of books available – there is no need to spend a fortune, just a few pounds per employee.

How to create service 'superstars' – training and career development

In addition to selecting the wrong people, one of the other problems often seen in all customer service roles relates to staff not understanding either the organization they work for or the products or services they offer. This can lead to them missing a potential customer issue that they encounter in a customer contact, whether by telephone, email or chat. We have already identified that one of the key elements that customers regard as part of good service is product knowledge (and any other information pertinent to the customer issue, such as environmental or operational changes).

In order to create anything approaching service 'super-stardom' for your team, training must incorporate not just skills training, but also organization and product knowledge. Fujitsu, the managed service provider, who won the SDI 'Service Desk of the Year' award in 2009, surround their first-line service people with a complete knowledge and information infrastructure to give them the best chance of being able to resolve a customer issue.

Ongoing training and career development to build on the attributes your people bring to the job is essential. Staff members at first direct have at least nine weeks' training when they join, and there is a system of coaching in place that ensures they operate at the highest level possible. That may not be possible or affordable for smaller organizations, but every organization must find its own way to develop its customer service.

A 2009 survey of nearly 1,000 business leaders, carried out by the IoD (Institute of Directors), revealed that despite the recession the investment in staff training was maintained or even increased in 8 out of 10 organizations over the six months to May 2009. IoD members identified the principal benefits of investing in training as: improved staff morale (76 per cent); improved productivity and/or profitability (74 per cent); improved customer satisfaction (69 per cent); and improved staff retention (62 per cent). Thirty-seven per cent believed that investing in training resulted in improved market share, and 21 per cent believed that it improved staff recruitment. Almost half (46 per cent) of employers said that they were focusing more on 'essential' training – short courses designed to meet immediate business needs, for example customer service training and sales training (IoD, 2009).

If you can select and recruit the right people and ensure that they are motivated, they will generally be keen to improve on their skills and knowledge to both progress their own career and also to become customer service 'superstars'. The challenge is to work out which of the many customer service training options to choose. There is so much publicly available – if you Google 'customer service training' there are 209 million sites to choose from – that it is worth spending some time working on what you want to achieve and then narrowing down your selection criteria. My recommendation is to go back to the customer service model you created in Chapter 3 – confirm your vision of the level of service you want and then devise the training and career development plan to achieve it consistently with the people you have.

Your training plan should of course take into account each person's aspirations for their career, their current level of skills and attributes and where you want them to be relative to your service model. Giving each staff member a personal development plan (PDP) is also good practice and should be reviewed at regular one-to-one performance reviews. In larger organizations you may want to develop a skills matrix of people and skills/attributes existing with a gap analysis to identify shortfalls.

Case study 7: Fujitsu

Fujitsu has several options available to staff to develop their skills and their career options. However, just being available is not enough. They go on to encourage their use through: assessment and development centres; a modern apprenticeships programme; career fairs; a corporate career mapping tool; coaching and/or mentoring programmes; a talent management programme; the emerging leaders programme; and the 'Fujitsu University', which offers staff a range of both internal and external training programmes.

In a specially developed customer care workbook, they highlight desired Fujitsu service behaviours both pictorially and in words:

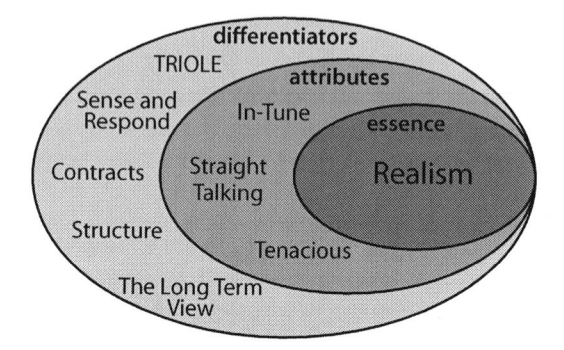

Diagram: TRIOLE model with concentric ellipses showing — differentiators (Sense and Respond, Contracts, Structure, The Long Term View); attributes (In-Tune, Straight Talking, Tenacious); essence (Realism)

- *We take ownership*: Relationships are personal. We each take personal ownership for our actions and see things through.
- *We act wisely*: Relationships are built on trust. We use our good judgement, always considering the impact of our actions today and in the future.
- *We make it simple*: Relationships require understanding. We take time to make the complex clear.
- *We stretch ourselves*: Relationships need to grow. We strive to do better for our customers and our colleagues every day.
- *We succeed together*: Relationships flourish when we work together. Across the whole business, we think and act as one.

(Fujitsu Service SDI Award Entry, 2009)

Once you have a sound idea of where you are relative to your model and vision, you can confidently decide what training and development is required to improve or maintain levels of service. Although the Fujitsu options highlighted in the case study above (such as the 'Fujitsu University') might not be feasible for many, especially smaller organizations, as with everything else, your options will be governed by the time and budget you can dedicate to training for your customer service people. The good news is that excellent results can be achieved at all spend levels, and the gain normally is in direct proportion to the ability of the training to engage the interest of the student. The main options available to you are listed below:

- *Employee and manager-led development.* This can be accomplished using books and either e-learning courses or other material available on the internet. It can be supplemented by on-the-job training and one-to-one coaching or mentoring time with an experienced manager, 'buddy' or mentor. This could include an analysis of recorded or past customer interactions. This is generally a low cost way and with the great books and material available works well as a full or part solution. There are several sources of study for great customer service in this book alone.
- *Internal or external training courses.* These can come with or without a qualification path. They can be conducted via an e-learning or classroom environment, or even a blend of the two, and role-playing exercises are often involved. These courses tend to be mid-range in cost, from a few hundred to a few thousand pounds depending on numbers, sector, qualification, reputation and brand. Industry associations, such as the Institute of Customer Service, SDI, Customer Contact Association (CCA), People 1st and the British Hospitality Association (BHA) all have vocational qualifications and can advise on the best options for you and your people. Some courses and qualifications are eligible for government funding support.
- *Customer service 'transformation programmes'.* Mary Gober pioneered the 'Gober Method', which is used by many – typically larger – organizations to effect a root and branch change to customer service attitudes, culture and delivery. It involves initial research and client understanding, and then a combination of training and coaching programmes for all levels of staff. These types of programme are also available from the larger consultancies such as Accenture, PA Consulting and IBM. All are reassuringly expensive, typically from tens of thousands to hundreds of thousands of pounds.
- *Simulations.* Another option that is employed is the use of actors in simulated customer experience interactions. Companies such as Power Train and Actors in Industry specialize in their provision.

Whichever option you choose, remember it is not a short-term campaign – it is the ongoing improvement of one of your most important business tools: your people.

The right organization structure

How do you balance a supportive environment for the retention and development of staff with the need to deliver great and consistent levels of service for customers?

To arrive at the right answer, you need to analyse what you have decided for your customer service model and service levels, as well as the processes (see Chapter 5 for more detail) that you will need to fulfil them. This will give you the opportunity to tune your structural template to fit your organization. The best way I have found to confirm the structure that would work best is to approach your industry association and ask them to refer you to an organization from their membership that is similar in size, customer base and services offered who would be happy for you to visit them and tell you how their structure works. You can then learn from their good – and bad – experiences for your model.

There are several factors that will influence your choice of customer facing structure, and these will vary depending on the type of industry you are in, but broadly it breaks down into the following tiers of service:

- *First-line customer service.* In a retail environment, whether a bank, supermarket or clothing or electrical store, this is provided by the shop-floor staff, who are responsible for advising and selling to customers, and taking their money. In a contact centre, it will be the staff who handle first-level customer calls or emails for sales or service enquiries. They will be equipped to handle most product enquiries and early stage customer dissatisfaction and complaints. If they are unable to resolve a query or complaint, the customer is passed onto second-line support.
- *Second-line support.* In retail, this is often the store manager or department head; in a contact centre or service desk, it could be the manager or product specialist, or a member of a specialist customer service department. These people will handle the enquiries, calls, emails and complaints that are unable to be resolved at the first line. Generally they will take the responsibility for providing the customer solution and feedback. If it is a particularly complex, technical or high-value customer issue it may require escalation to third-line support.
- *Third-line support.* In all organizations, this will typically be senior product specialists, senior managers or directors. If a customer issue gets this far, then it is serious, and it will either be risking the loss of business, or more critically, the customer. At this level, the decisions made to resolve the issue will need to balance the cost of the remedy with the longer-term loss potential of this and possibly other customers.

The three-tier structure works well for customers and can be adapted to most types of organization, requiring typically only minor adjustment. It should be borne in mind that the earlier you resolve the issue, the less it costs.

It is fair to expect in the region of 80 per cent of the contacts to be resolved at the first level. The typical handling cost of first-line contact in a service desk environment would be in the region of £1–£15 depending on whether it was handled by self-service, email or telephone without any further cost of repair or replacement added. For the cost of handling beyond the first line for each tier, you can multiply that cost by a factor of between five and 10, depending on the type of issue and organization, bearing in mind the additional time, number and cost of people to be involved. If a customer query or complaint gets to the level of CEO or product guru, the cost can be vast, even ignoring the potential lifetime value issues.

Employee satisfaction and support

You should now have a good indication of how to structure for delivering to customers, but what are the organizational considerations to provide the right team environment? A supportive team environment will help smooth transition and restrict conflict between the tiers (many first-line customer service teams report patchy rapport with and response from second- and third-line staff) and also help staff to feel supported and valued, thereby increasing levels of staff retention.

Bruce Temkin (2009) advised 'To embed customer experience within the core operating fabric of a company, a firm needs to refine what it measures, incentivises, and celebrates. So make sure that your HR exec is involved in the customer experience effort' – which is good advice and will ensure you know what you can use to create the balanced structure you need for both customers and staff.

Some of the things that organizations implement to add to the training and career development of staff are benefits such as gyms or crèches. Vertex, the contact centre organization, has a fitness initiative called 'Let's Get Healthy' which helps staff to check health indicators and eat well. first direct and O2 provide staff transport to city centres, and many organizations now have on-site coffee shops and staff restaurants which double as informal relaxing and meeting areas. At BA and first direct there are even shops built into their office complexes.

Many larger organizations run independent employee satisfaction surveys that not only give you the chance to gauge how happy your people are but also give you the chance to find out about other related factors. 'HCL Employee First' is now a recognized philosophy which does exactly that. *Fortune Magazine* has articulated it as 'The World's Most Modern Management' and it is a case study at Harvard Business School (HCL, 2009).

The concept of 'Employee First, Customer Second' at India's HCL Technologies arises out of the belief that it is employees who create value for customers, not top management, and thus need to be empowered. HCL started its transformation in 2005, the key challenge being that the employees were technically skilled and creative, but not motivated. The 'Employee First' philosophy – the first such articulation in the IT services industry – is at the core of all efforts to provide employees with a work environment and culture that they can take pride in, recognizing that the employee interface with the customer is crucial. Through this initiative, HCL strives to provide excellent HR leadership and expertise, to attract and retain a workforce that is diverse, inclusive and committed to creating quality customer service. HCL's enlightened approach to employee development focuses on giving people whatever they need to succeed: be it a virtual assistant or talent transformation sabbaticals; expert guidance or fast-track growth; inner peace or democratic empowerment. For this, HCL has adopted a fivefold path to individual enlightenment – support, knowledge, recognition, empowerment and transformation. The four stated objectives of Employee First are to:

- create a unique employee experience – a 'wow' feeling;
- invert the organizational structure;
- enhance transparency and accountability;
- learn – grow – own.

(HCL, 2009)

A good team environment will see staff consulted and contributing, thanked when doing well and helped when they are not. The SDI standards specify the features of a good team and its environment:

> An effective team: has clear goals/objectives; has effective communication skills; is empowered to make decisions; displays a sense of participation; has higher productivity; has high morale and motivation; has multiple/various skills; has effective conflict resolution policies; has a unified commitment and meets agreed objectives and targets.

> A typical friendly and supportive workplace has a good and visible rapport among team members who have an interest in each other's development; is empowered by management; shows a team willingness to collaborate with and assist other team members; has responsible and trustworthy team members; has a diverse blend of team members.

> (SDI service desk manager standards, 2009)

This supportive workplace is often more important than the salary and benefits, which diminish as motivators over time. It requires work to achieve this type of environment and for the culture you set to be right, but is much less costly to achieve than paying people more or giving extensive staff benefits. Often a bag of doughnuts as a team thank-you or a spontaneous social evening can be more valued than formal company-wide benefit schemes.

When staff feel supported and valued, they are often more willing to contribute ideas and suggestions for the company. In Accenture's online *Outlook* journal, David Smith and Craig Mindrum's article 'How to capture the essence of innovation' (2008) noted that 'the key to successful innovation is an internal network that actively involves people throughout the organization in the vibrancy of discovery and dialogue, and provides the means to distil the fruits of that dialogue into value-generating ideas.' The internal network that they refer to is effectively the modern equivalent of the 'suggestions box', recognizing that most ideas are generated by people – and especially those directly related to the task in hand. Encouraging people to contribute is crucial and the supportive environment will clearly help and may in turn unearth the idea that makes a big difference to the organization, as Smith and Mindrum (2008) go on to say:

> Creating such an innovation network – a two-way flow of learning and ideation that is both abundant and relevant – is every bit as crucial to sustained high performance as an IT breakthrough or the launch of a game-changing new product.

This can apply across any size of organization and include staff in multiple or global sites. It can also be used to drive new levels of collaboration, an essential aspect of business today, and help to spread knowledge and new ways of working, helping to ease the 'pain' of continual change that is a fixture in most businesses now.

Self-service?

In a chapter about customer service people, it might seem a little odd to discuss service without them. However, in *The Best Service is No Service* (Price and Jaffe, 2008) there is a heavy emphasis on the elimination of 'dumb' contacts – i.e. where there is little or no value in the customer speaking to a person. That Bill Price was previously the customer service director at Amazon might come as no surprise, but the point gives us a great direction for the use of customer self-service tools. The simple transaction options found to be most convenient in the survey by Invomo (2009) are information/brochure requests, competitions and store finders (Table 1).

Table 1. Convenient transaction options (Invomo, 2009).

	Average rating	Most convenient (4–5 rating)
Request brochure	3.6	56%
Enter competition	3.5	55%
Nearest store	3.5	54%
Bank balance	3.3	47%
Mailing list add/remove	3.2	45%
Order status	3.1	43%
Change of address	2.8	34%

High levels of self-service technology combined with a knowledgebase can make significant cost savings, even if only 15 per cent of employees are willing and able to use the knowledge-enabled self-service, which is a typical usage percentage for self-service options. It must be remembered, however, that there is no such thing as a free lunch; other factors, including the initial investment in the knowledge management solution, will affect overall return on investment (ROI). Nevertheless, where the full cost of handling a customer call may be £10–15 when office, benefit and other costs are taken into account, with the average online answer costing £1, the savings can be immense, often running into thousands of pounds per month.

You need to consider, of course, whether these tools and processes are right for your service model and customers. Customer service is ultimately about people: using technology to help people get better – or quicker – service is fine as long as your customers accept it as a valid option and you are able to replicate or beat the good service your staff members are able to give.

Should you put your people before your customers?

The Harvard Service Profit Chain discussed in Chapter 3 shows that there is a direct connection between employee satisfaction, customer satisfaction and an organization's financial performance. Without committed, service-oriented employees you are unlikely to be able to deliver consistently great customer service. Accenture's *Leadership in Customer Service: Delivering on the Promise* report suggests a transformation programme if it is felt that staff cannot meet the needs of the citizens they serve or support (Accenture, 2007).

People do make the difference when it comes to service. You should be investing just as much time and effort in looking after your staff as you do your customers; put them on an equal footing. In the organizations with a reputation for great service, the people who work there typically think that it is a good or nice place to work, so logically it follows that the happier people are with the organization they work for, the more likely they are to deliver great service to customers.

Summary

People clearly do make the difference when it comes to service, and the factors we have highlighted in this chapter will help you to recruit and select the right people and build them into your team to deliver great customer service. It should be noted that none of the sections here are stand-alone; they need to work together and link to your chosen customer service model and vision.

There are some basics to get right: job descriptions, deciding which strengths, skills and attributes you are looking for, and creating the right organization structure and team environment, but perhaps the most important to remember is the application of leadership and management to ignite passion and emotion and keep people motivated.

Alongside this, you will need to train and develop people in line with the aspiration to meet your service model and vision – which is not a short-term campaign, but an ongoing task – and choose a programme according to your budget, spending only what you can afford to get the best you can.

Learning points

Getting the team balance right and getting the team working well together is often the biggest customer service challenge, but they reap significant rewards.

The most important points to remember are listed below:

- Understand your customer service model and vision and select and recruit the people who will fit.
- Create a list of strengths, skills and attributes you are looking for and test for them in your recruiting process. (SDI professional standards give comprehensive guidance on the skills, attributes and behaviours required.)

- Use BS 8477 to guide your team building, but do not use obligations to try to motivate your staff – use softer, culturally driven methods.
- Use your CEO or other senior champion to help you to inspire and to apply the culture, passion and motivation you need.
- Input an element of fun into the day-to-day work and training of your staff, but not to the detriment of achieving your business objectives.
- Adapt the 'three tier' service structure to your own organization for a tried and tested model.
- If you are using a self-service structure, make sure that it has a human feel.

The following is a short list of techniques and examples to consider and learn from.

Techniques:

- Bruce Temkin advised involving your HR exec to ensure you know what you can use to create the balanced structure you need for both customers and staff.
- Turning on the motivational switch and igniting the passions and emotions of your people is one of the most written about areas in business. But it also occurs in other fields – we gave the examples of Manchester United football club and Ben Zander with his orchestras. Can you mirror the 'winning' of other types of team in your own team?
- Can you apply the motivational methods captured by Di Kamp on our SDI workshop, whose list of ideas such as 'five things to make a difference to my or my team's motivation' and the ability to set clear values and have fun, make people feel valued and trusted in a supportive work environment?
- Encouraging your staff to contribute, being a visible leader, consulting your team about decisions, catching them doing something right and praising them, and communicating with and understanding your team completely are all principles for leadership espoused by David Taylor in his book *The Naked Leader*.

Examples:

- Fujitsu's Sense and Respond uses service desk 'intelligence' to identify common issues across the customer base and/or issues that have a high impact on a customer's business. This enables the desk to move towards proactive behaviour rather than receiving the customer call after an incident has occurred. The Sense and Respond approach is underpinned through a central practice which trains service desk teams in data gathering, analysis, process improvement and customer contact habits as well as future innovation ideas.

- Amazon does great self-service, but also keeps the human 'feel' to its service: you can do this too.
- HCL's 'Employee First' cultural philosophy to support employees in turn supports the Harvard Service Profit Chain principle by investing in staff to in turn deliver service to customers.

5

Customer service processes

Process as our foundation

I have already outlined the best structure for delivering service to reflect the priority of the customer. Linked to this was the need to build 'tiers' of customer service – with clear responsibilities at each tier – using best practice processes and procedures. The three tiers identified were first-, second- and third-line customer service and support.

Each of these tiers will be examined in greater detail, and I will identify the key processes that should be in place to ensure that the great service you are aiming to provide has the best possible chance of being achieved consistently, despite any changes in the personnel involved, the technology deployed or the ever changing nature of business today. Establishing the right set of processes and then ensuring that your team is well trained in them so that they operate as second nature is the bedrock of consistently successful service. This chapter, although perhaps less exciting than chapters on customer experience or technology, is actually the most important.

BS 8477 *Code of Practice for Customer Service*, places great emphasis on customer service processes in its implementation advice – 'management should be responsible for empowering front-line employees with the information, resources and authority to meet customer needs to own and solve customer problems, to ensure there is a process to require subcontractors to support the organization's customer culture, and a process in place to escalate and report on customer service problems' – and there is much more in the standard that will contribute to the successful implementation of your service processes. For example it provides guidance on information and documentation requirements, both essential aspects, for different types of customer interaction. These will be referred to throughout this chapter.

What do I need to remember to succeed?

Perhaps the most important thing to remember at this stage is that whatever processes you choose to fit your own unique operation, they will need regular updates and tuning as your business and customers evolve. You should be continually watching for factors that could impact on the delivery of great service; just as you review the performance of your people, you will need to do the same with processes to feed your service improvement plans. BS 8477 advises 'to ensure there is a procedure in place to review all customer service processes regularly'. This should be done (formally) at least annually in addition to the interim informal review and tuning that should occur.

The other major factor to bear in mind at this stage is the 'closed loop' requirement of customer service processes. 'Closing the loop' simply means getting back to the point at which the process started, with a closure or solution and the relevant feedback information. This is an often reported failure point in customer service, with either the solution or customer feedback missing or not communicated. As we identified earlier, this is a major cause of customer dissatisfaction, has a significant effect on loyalty and adds to the cost of service, either generating a complaint that then has to be handled or losing the customer altogether. The process flow that Motability uses (Figure 10) is a simple example that shows the progression from first contact to closure, for a first-line customer (user) request or problem. One of the excellent features of this flowchart is that it shows the approval of the customer as part of the closure process.

You will see that, before closure, the customer (user) is consulted. This information (in addition to the closure and internal information on how that was achieved) on the solution (or if not possible, some other options to help) and how it affects the customer is essential. This point reinforces the need to document the detail as well as showing the flow of processes so that it is clear what needs to be accomplished at each stage. It is also worth remembering that the customer will be the start and endpoint of interactions in all but a few cases.

You will also have noted that both process flows refer to resolution at tier 2 or 2.5 in the case of Motability with reference to specialist support group, which could indicate that escalation to third-line support is to be avoided at all costs. Whatever the definition, the closed-loop process is a priority to ensure that the customer leaves the process at least satisfied, but preferably having experienced the great service that will ensure their long-term loyalty.

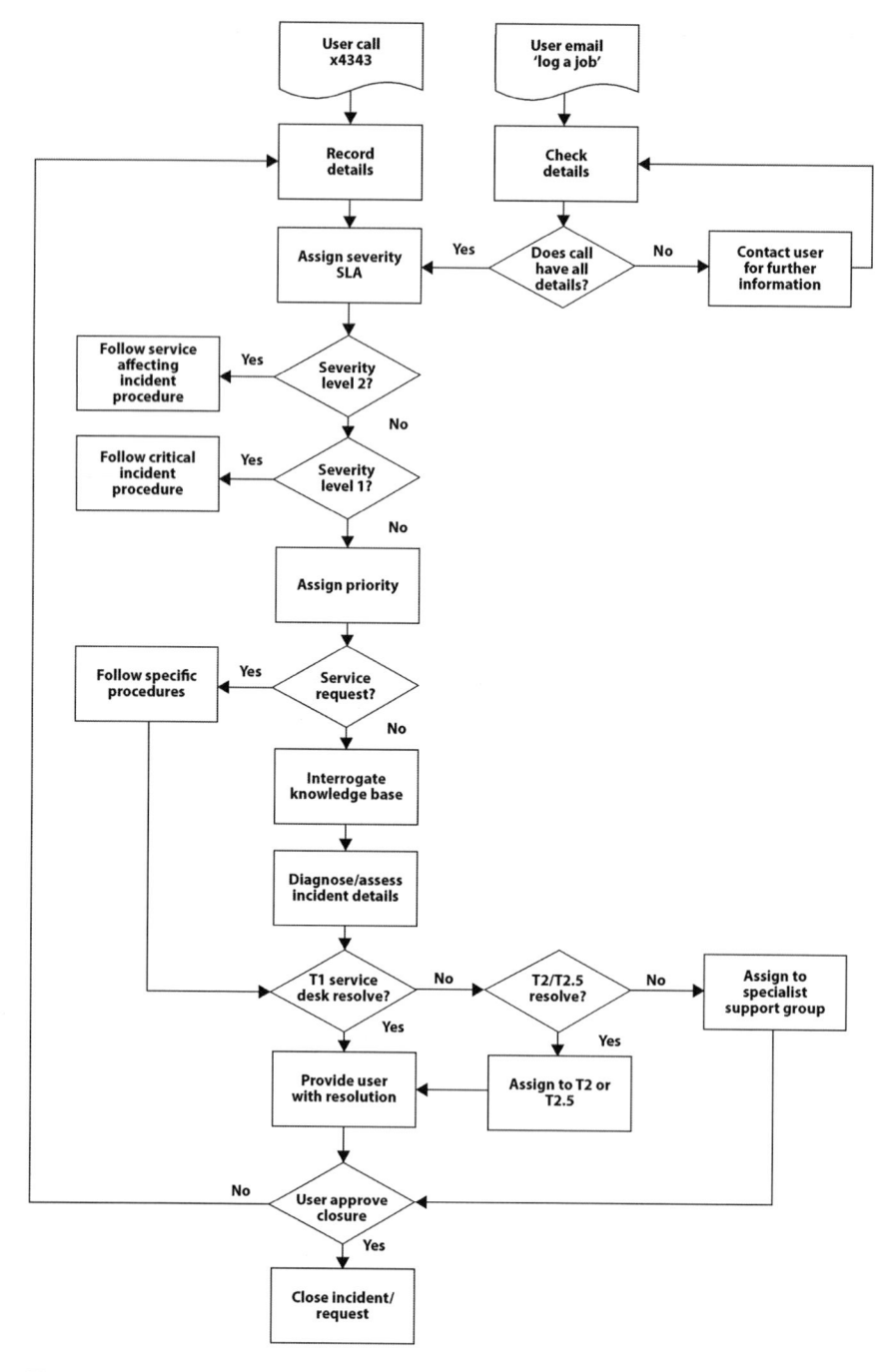

Figure 10. Motability Operations service desk (James Davis, Service Desk Manager September, 2008).

First-line customer service

You will recall from Chapter 1 that the Institute of Customer Service research report *Customer Priorities* (2006) gives a simple 'top 10' list of priorities: overall quality of the product or service supplied; friendliness of staff; handling problems and complaints; speed of service; helpfulness of staff; handling enquiries; being treated as a valued customer; competence of staff; ease of doing business; being kept informed. The majority of these concern stages of the 'customer handling' processes that will be covered in this chapter – and most of these are related to first-line contact.

Your first consideration is that you should aim to *prevent* the customer needing to get to this first line – and certainly beyond it – at all. If you can adopt preventive measures and reduce the number of contacts that the customer needs to make with you, then the cost of handling fewer contacts will of course be lower. If the contact is not preventable, you need to make every effort to resolve the issue on the first contact to save the additional cost for you (and delay for the customer) of going beyond the first line. If this in turn is not possible, it is important that the ownership of the customer issue is clear in order for it not to 'fall down the cracks' in the process and that someone is responsible for 'closing the loop'. This will invariably involve providing the customer with the solution, and in most organizations sits best at the first line of service as they typically possess the best customer skills.

Price and Jaffe's book, *The Best Service Is No Service* (2008), has the subtitle 'how to liberate your customers from customer service, keep them happy and control costs'. Although you could challenge the subtitle's assumption that customers want to be liberated, the authors make the point (in their seven principles to move to 'best service') that challenging the customer demand for service and eliminating 'dumb contacts' will allow you to focus on the other areas of importance, such as delivering a great customer experience. Figure 11 offers an illustration of those seven principles.

You need to assess *all* of the first-line contacts that you have with customers to see which are necessary and which are desirable – based on an analysis of both customer need and desire. You should also assess whether the information or contact need can be achieved in another way to eliminate the 'dumb contacts'. This could be by directing customers to product information on a website, sending distributors of our products better information to display in store or offering answers to frequently asked questions (FAQs).

The Best Service Is No Service

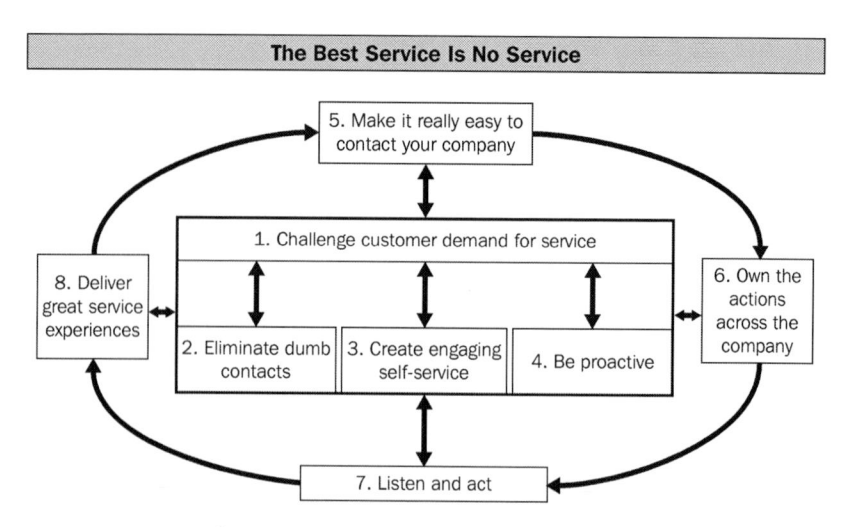

```
                    5. Make it really easy to
                        contact your company

                  1. Challenge customer demand for service

8. Deliver                                                      6. Own the
great service                                                   actions
experiences    2. Eliminate dumb   3. Create engaging            across the
               contacts            self-service   4. Be proactive company

                          7. Listen and act
```

Figure 11. The best service is no service (Price and Jaffe, 2008).

This task and how it is carried out will depend, of course, on the type of business you are and the nature of customer interactions and contacts that you have. For example, the assessment of customer contacts in a retail store environment will involve spending time in store evaluating both the nature and extent of customer interaction with store staff. This gives a first-hand opportunity to experience exactly what the customer does and is often undertaken using mystery shoppers, either employed by the organization or by a specialist agency.

Whether or not you choose to use mystery shoppers, the power of the information that you can gain from customers – before they buy or initiate the first contact and the contact itself – is immense. In many of the 'best' businesses, the chief executive and senior managers or directors frequently spend time in their own stores or contact centres serving customers or simply observing activity and customer behaviour. This 'back to the floor' approach was made famous in the BBC series of the same name in the late 1990s. Feargal Quinn, owner of the Irish supermarket chain 'SuperQuinn', speaking at a customer service conference I ran around that time was a big advocate of this process. He recounted one story where, when acting as a bag-packer himself, he noticed a very efficient checkout and went over to congratulate the woman on how efficiently she had handled the customer. 'Just one thing, though, you forgot to say thank you.' 'No need, it's written on the bottom of the receipt' was her response. Needless to say he emphasized the need to make the 'thank you' a little more personal and updated cashier training to include that guidance.

Mystery shopping is an established way of determining the quality of customer experiences and can also be used to assess other interactions if the business is not a store-based retailer. Where the vast majority of business is conducted online or through the post or on the telephone, mystery shopping can still be used. Whether you employ others to do this contact assessment task or whether you choose to do it yourself (most likely in smaller or budget-restricted organizations), it is crucial that you assess each type of actual or potential customer contact, depending on your environment. Customers will generally have a relatively limited range of types of interaction requirement – wanting to buy your products or services, asking about them, reporting a problem or complaint, asking how to use or get help using them, or reporting an incident or emergency. Unless you are able to assess the likely balance of these types of interaction in your business, it will be difficult to determine the skills and training that staff need – and make it more difficult to establish successful processes.

Legislation and consumer rights

Whatever the size of your organization, there are a number of legislative and simple good sense issues to be aware of relating to fair trading and consumer protection laws. They need to be borne in mind throughout the customer service process, and organizations should be up to date with any changes. A good source of guidance is the Office of Fair Trading website (www.oft.gov.uk) which has a downloadable guide to the latest (2007) laws in the area. There is a more wide-ranging set of guidance at the Department of Business, Enterprise and Regulatory Reform website (www.berr.gov.uk/).

Particular issues to consider are whether some customers might need help to access your products or services (and get support/service for them) because of, for example, disability or language barriers. There is legislation to cover some of the requirements, but commercial considerations may make it good sense to ensure that all customers are able to gain access to your business. For example Post Offices use induction hearing loops to help them to serve deaf customers. The RNID (Royal National Institute for the Deaf) has a wide range of devices and guidance for deaf people at www.rnid.org.uk. Similar guidance for other forms of impairment is widely available on the internet or from the respective support organizations.

Customer service charters and service level agreements

When researching and developing your model for customer service you may have come across charters and service level agreements (SLAs). The latter is most commonly used in IT services, but both can appear in all spheres of service. Put simply, both are non-binding commitments by an organization to deliver a level of service to another organization or individual consumer. A typical example of a charter is given in Case study 9, and you will notice that although it is good in committing to, for example, being 'efficient, effective and accessible, honest, open and accountable', and commits to continual improvement, it does not have specific targets to achieve, other than publishing an annual statement on customer service. SLAs on the other hand, usually contain specific targets for the service provider to achieve or a clear parameter within which the service will operate.

Case study 9: Big Lottery customer service charter

Who we are and what we do

This customer service charter sets out the service you can expect. If you have any particular communication needs, or need information in other languages or format, please contact the lottery distributor you are dealing with.

Customer service principles

We aim to:

- consider the views of our customers;
- be efficient, effective and accessible; be honest, open and accountable for our actions;
- provide clear and appropriate information, guidance and feedback;
- share and learn from best practice in order to continually improve the service we offer;
- publish an annual statement on customer service.

All the lottery distributors have agreed to use the same process for reviewing complaints. If you have a complaint about the service you have received from one of the lottery distributors, please contact them direct.

(www.biglotteryfund.org.uk/pub_cust_charter.pdf , undated)

The following example from JANET (UK) (2009), which provides a support service giving advice and technical guidance to organizations on roaming network access, issues and maintains appropriate terms for organizations using the service:

The support service is available during Support Working Hours.

Service Specific Definitions

Support Working Days are Working Days excluding the Easter Bank Holiday Monday, the last Monday in August, and the period of 24 to 31 December (inclusive).

Support Working Hours are 09:00–17:00 on Support Working Days.

Service Levels:

a) Service Availability will be 99.5% for the national RADIUS [service].
b) Access to the national RADIUS…service for an organisation will be enabled within 15 Support Working Days of receipt of all necessary information and the organisation's completion of configuring their RADIUS [service].
c) An initial response to any enquiry will be given within four Support Working Hours.'

(JANET (UK) www.ja.net/documents/publications/policy/sla.pdf, 2009)

The two contrasting examples above will both influence the expectation of customers on the outcome of customer service processes, and both are valid tools to deploy to manage that expectation. However, you will need to decide whether either is appropriate in conjunction with your normal contracts and terms and conditions of sale. It is advisable to consult with your steering group if you have one, or to ask the advice of organizations of similar size.

I believe that if you are offering simple retail products for sale, the service charter may be the most appropriate, whereas if you have relatively constant or complex services that you provide, an SLA will be the best to use. In either case they should reflect the service culture of the organization and be used as a means to build relationships with customers. Above all, they should be simple – as per this charter from Virgin Trains:

Virgin Trains – Passenger Charter

This is the Passenger's Charter for West Coast Trains Ltd, which operates under the name of 'Virgin Trains'. It sets out our commitment to give you the safe, high quality service you have the right to expect. Any passenger purchasing a ticket for use on services operated by Virgin Trains should enjoy:

- a reliable and punctual journey
- clean and safe trains and stations
- a Customer Service team member onboard each train to be available to provide help if required
- a refreshment service on most trains; a seat if reserved in advance.

(www.virgintrains.co.uk/docs/PASSENGERS_CHARTER_11_NOV_2007.pdf,2007)

First-line customer interaction methods

We have examined some of the issues that could define, influence or govern the first-line customer service interface. That should all condition the way you prepare for the ways in which you will interact with your customers. The other factor that is important is that customers will demand a choice – they may wish to use one, two or even all of these methods of contact. Although you may not wish, or be able, to offer them all, it is important that customers receive consistently good service whichever option they choose.

Today's world of electronic communications offers a wide choice of communication methods. No longer are we able to offer *just* postal and telephone services, we are now committed to providing one or all of email-, internet- and chat-based services in many cases. Social media is the latest electronic communication method to arrive, but I firmly believe that, until it establishes itself as a mainstream and profitable format for purposes other than principally personal, social and community information sharing, it has no place yet in direct customer service processes. I do see the potential for using it for brand image and marketing awareness and development (and for monitoring possible complaint and negative brand commentary). We will address the possible service uses of social media in Chapter 6.

The main methods of communication today and in the foreseeable future will be post, telephone, email, internet and chat, and these will be the primary options chosen by customers. The Invomo 2009 study quoted in Chapter 4 showed that 39 per cent of the customers surveyed chose to make purchases by calling contact centres rather than buying online (47 per cent of over 55 year olds); over two-thirds wanted detailed information before buying; and others cited difficulty in using online ordering or finding calling more convenient or having more confidence in talking to someone.

A further factor that makes customers wary of using any method of remote buying is security. The rise in identity theft or credit card fraud has meant that in the survey, between 64 and 73 per cent of customers were concerned about the possibility of a security issue arising; hence our challenge of achieving a secure and service-oriented first-line customer service point is significant. Although security is not the subject of this book, BSI has developed standards and guidance documents regarding data protection online, which help to ensure compliance in this area. (They are, specifically, BS 10012 *Data protection – Specification for a personal information management system* and BIP 0050 *Data Protection Pocket Guide: Essential Facts at Your Fingertips*.)

The modern contact centre option, often the option of choice for larger businesses, with all customer contacts routed through one department in the business, has the advantage of making all customer contacts the responsibility of one manager or group of managers. It will be their responsibility to ensure that the customer receives and, perhaps more importantly, perceives that they receive the service level that the business has decided. It is also their responsibility to ensure that the organization achieves the service in the most efficient and cost-effective manner. In the best organizations (e.g. Amazon and first direct) this is achieved, and both the organization and the customer are happy. In organizations where this does not work effectively, it exposes the potential shortfalls of this centralization of customer contact. These shortfalls include the lack of involvement of other teams who become remote and disinterested in customer matters and the difficulty of communication between the contact centre and other teams who may be operating in different cultures and time zones. There is also the view of the customer that they cannot speak to anyone who can really help to resolve their issue.

In organizations in which customer contact can be kept more personal or face to face, the interaction is generally easier to manage if you have the right customer-oriented staff who are also well trained, simply because the customer will be standing in front of them or will liaise with them in person more often. In a large contact centre a customer may never speak to the same person twice, and if they buy online they may never speak to anyone.

In the following example, Sony's online entertainment business (SOE) recognized that their customers primarily contacted them online or through email, but they still had a significant amount of telephone traffic. They worked with a technology supplier to adopt an integrated contact centre solution to draw together all customer contacts and improve customer and problem solution knowledge. Figure 12 shows the workflow before and after the change.

86　*Quality Service, Competitive Business: setting the standard in customer service*

Sony Online Entertainment (SOE) migrated from a fragmented set of applications to an integrated and on demand customer service solution by RightNow that provides a complete customer view, a multi-channel customer contact center, and a single desktop for both in-house as well as outsourced agents. The customer and the agent experience improved—and, SOE saved an estimated $817,706 from 2004 through 2007.

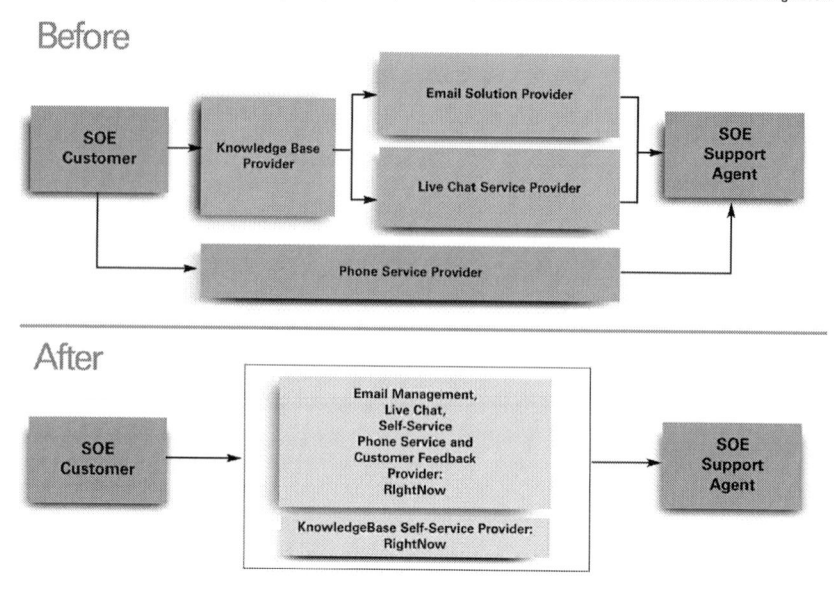

Before

```
                          ┌─→ Email Solution Provider ──┐
SOE Customer ──→ Knowledge Base Provider                ├──→ SOE Support Agent
                          └─→ Live Chat Service Provider ┘
              └─────────────→ Phone Service Provider ────────────┘
```

After

```
SOE Customer ──→ Email Management, Live Chat, Self-Service Phone Service and Customer Feedback Provider: RightNow ──→ SOE Support Agent
                 KnowledgeBase Self-Service Provider: RightNow
```

Figure 12. The evolution of customer service (SOE, 2009).

As you can see, the solution also met the criteria for being very cost-effective. Mapping out your processes to handle each of the customer contact methods and how you will answer them is a sensible way to visualize how they will work. You will need to decide whether to handle different types of contact, or even different types of customer grouping, into different teams – for example, many contact centres separate telephone contact and written contacts such as email and post, and some scan post into electronic formats so that it can all be handled electronically within the business. Chat or instant messaging contacts could be handled in a separate department again – or by the 'written' team. Chat is no longer considered to be a costly 'extra' customer service channel, and skilled staff can sometimes handle several chats simultaneously in the time it can take to handle a single phone call. Chat can help to engage customers and keep them on your website or guide customers through online form filling and any technical support. Chat has the advantage of staff being able to 'see' what customers are doing, which aids first-line resolution.

Email has grown significantly to become the predominant written customer communication. When a customer sends you an email, they expect to receive a quick and relevant response. If they do not, they are likely to phone or email again, which increases customer frustration and staff workload, which in turn increases your costs. It is important to adopt some form of service level to govern customer expectation in this regard, usually now expected within hours as opposed to the days 'allowed' by customers for postal communication. Many organizations now use email response technology to both acknowledge receipt of the customer email and prompt a meaningful response to meet the committed response level. This will be covered further in Chapter 6.

Most organizations make some sort of commitment to responding to email or post within, say, 24 hours; telephone and chat are, of course, 'instant' (where technology allows). A particular complaint from customers is queuing time on automated phone systems – two to three minutes is generally considered to be the maximum a customer is willing to wait. (Further information on the telephone options available will be covered in Chapter 6.) It is acceptable for your method of contact to be faster than the method chosen by customers, but if your choice begins to affect customer satisfaction or service adversely, you may wish to reassess and possibly change the options at your next review point.

Case study 10: Chiltern District Council's key performance standards

- To respond to 95% of all telephone calls within 20 seconds (6 rings) and to return all calls the next working day. If we cannot give you a satisfactory reply when you telephone we will call back at an agreed time.
- To respond to 80% of correspondence within 10 working days and 100% in 15 working days. If we cannot give a full reply within that time we will let you know when you can expect one and why there is a delay.
- We will always provide you with a contact name and number.
- Visitors to the Council Offices will be welcomed by the receptionist and all visitors will be seen by a customer services assistant within four minutes of being greeted by the receptionist.

These are minimum standards. Specific services may set standards that aim to exceed this corporate standard and will also set service specific standards relating to other aspects of their service.

(www.chiltern.gov.uk/site/scripts/documents_info.php?documentID=263&page Number=5, 2009)

Chiltern District Council has given their customers a simple expectation of when and how they will respond in these standards.

In a smaller organization *all* communication may be handled by the same person or group of people – making consistency and reaching a standard service level potentially easier. My recommendation, if possible, for organizations of any size, is to at least have all customer contacts made the responsibility of, and managed by, the same manager or team if you choose to have a central customer contact centre. If you do not make this choice, then the decision to split the handling of contact types in any way is secondary to this. This will help to achieve consistency – especially if a common response standard is adopted *whatever* type of customer contact is made.

In addition to the commitment to timeliness of response – which is essential to avoid customer dissatisfaction – you will also need to consider and address the consistency of the greeting and the way the contact is handled within the model and process you have selected. The potential to further irritate a customer already frustrated with a problem or complaint issue is high in all first-contact situations, and if you remove the face-to-face advantage of being able to see the customer's expressions then it becomes greater.

To that end, SDI qualification standards give first-line service desk staff guidance for using email. For example, using business style writing is essential, as is writing clear and concise messages. Using the correct punctuation and not using email for difficult or sensitive issues is good practice, as is using plain text and avoiding fancy fonts, colours and RTF- or HTML-specific formatting. You should avoid the use of abbreviations and emoticons and use standard headers or footers that are approved by management. The use of signature blocks and avoidance of single word or phrase responses (e.g. 'yes', 'I agree') is good practice. Including the original message with replies and avoiding the use of all upper case letters is best practice, as is taking time to check and review your email (SDI, 2007).

The standards also cover professional call handling:

> You should take care when listening to and understanding the customer description of the Incident or Service Request. You should try to address the emotional needs of the customer (i.e. be empathetic and probe for any clarification required). Speaking clearly and concisely and focusing on actions to resolve the customer's Incident or Service Request are good practice and you should always be using silent time effectively.
>
> (SDI Service Desk Analyst Qualification Standards, 2007)

These types of standards leave less room for error in first-line communications, and you should create your own versions using industry models as a template.

If the customer is expecting a resolution at the first contact, and most customers prefer solutions or the right information early in the contact, the expectation should be fulfilled as often as possible in the best *way* possible – not least because it costs your organization much more to pass the issue on to second line or beyond, but mainly because it increases customer satisfaction and loyalty.

First-line staff will require training to a high standard (addressed in Chapter 4), be empowered to take action to resolve customer issues (perhaps even with an authorized 'spend' level to boost resolutions), and be aware of likely customer behaviours and requirements, in addition to the policies and practices the organization would wish to encourage. First-line staff represent your organization entirely during the interaction with your customers. Hence your process should also identify when it is appropriate for the issue to be passed on to second-line support and how that should occur. In short, there should be guidance for contact prevention, receipt, handling, resolution or referral, closure and communication of the solution to customer and service improvement process.

For the first-line process, the key issues to address are – as a minimum – the assessment of why the customer might be calling and if there is anything you could have done to avoid their need to call. In addition you should specify how they will contact you – offering a choice of method with indicated response times – how you will handle the contact whatever method is chosen, and when to pass the issue to the second line. Also worth considering is what you can possibly handle without direct customer contact – probably online – and what you need to do to empower first-line staff to respond as you and customers would require.

Ensure that these guidelines are recorded in documentation or on a knowledgebase for staff to refresh their knowledge from time to time as well as feeding the service improvement process. Customers will also need to be informed of what they should expect and how they should contact you – BS 8477 subclause 5.2 offers comprehensive guidance on how this should be done in terms of content, timeliness and accessibility. The standard places particular emphasis on clarity: customers need to be guided to the right place first time to avoid causing frustration.

Second-line customer service and support

As indicated previously, it is preferable *not* to reach this point; if you do, it is usually indicative of a failure to prevent the contact, and the inability of your first-line service to resolve the issue. This could be for a number of reasons: lack of knowledge at the first line; the need to escalate a serious complaint or a major problem; or simply the customer insistence to 'speak to a manager'. In a small organization, the first point of contact may well be that manager, but if not, or if it is a larger organization, then it is still a failure of the first-line process to resolve the issue. Consideration should be given to reviewing the first-line interaction guidance to ensure this escalation occurs infrequently.

However, if it *is* a serious complaint or major problem, then the rapid application of specialist or senior expertise is desirable. This issue is now not only serious from the customer point of view but it is also distracting the staff involved from their core jobs of providing products or services to customers. The only good news that results from a customer issue reaching this stage is that it provides you with a good opportunity to improve the quality of your product or service, or your processes.

With the application of senior expertise you will be looking to resolve this issue with due haste to minimize the impact on both the customer and your organization. The best way to do this is to operate a method that allows the first line to identify rapidly the key people in the organization who can resolve customer issues within each particular area of the product or service portfolio. These second-line 'experts' should be listed, together with their areas of expertise, for the first-line team to enable them to achieve rapid escalation. The ownership of the customer issue, as identified earlier, should still remain with the first-line team as they have the best skills in customer interaction, so that they can ensure that the customer receives a response from whoever finally resolves the issue. Closing the loop in the customer service process, and automated customer issue tracking and management systems are invaluable in achieving this response.

Just as for the emergency services, many organizations operate a 'major incident procedure' as in the following example from Anchor Housing Trust (Figure 13).

Anchor's example relates to the IT services they offer to the many housing estates they support, but they use the procedure to ensure effective co-ordination of resources, customer information, escalation when appropriate and the closure of the incident with the solution details to aid ongoing service improvements.

Another method that is used to good effect with customer issues or complaints that are more serious or costly is that of the 'post-mortem'. Particularly effective in cases in which perhaps the issue is the first of its kind, it sets out to analyse constructively the issue and all of the things that occurred relating to its cause and resulting impact. The opinions of all of the people involved are also sought, and the aim is both to prevent the issue and its underlying causes occurring again and to learn any lessons that may be applied to improve products, services or processes. The key point of building knowledge is to both improve and also make the first line more able to handle a larger volume of customer issues.

Customer service processes 91

IS services major incident procedure

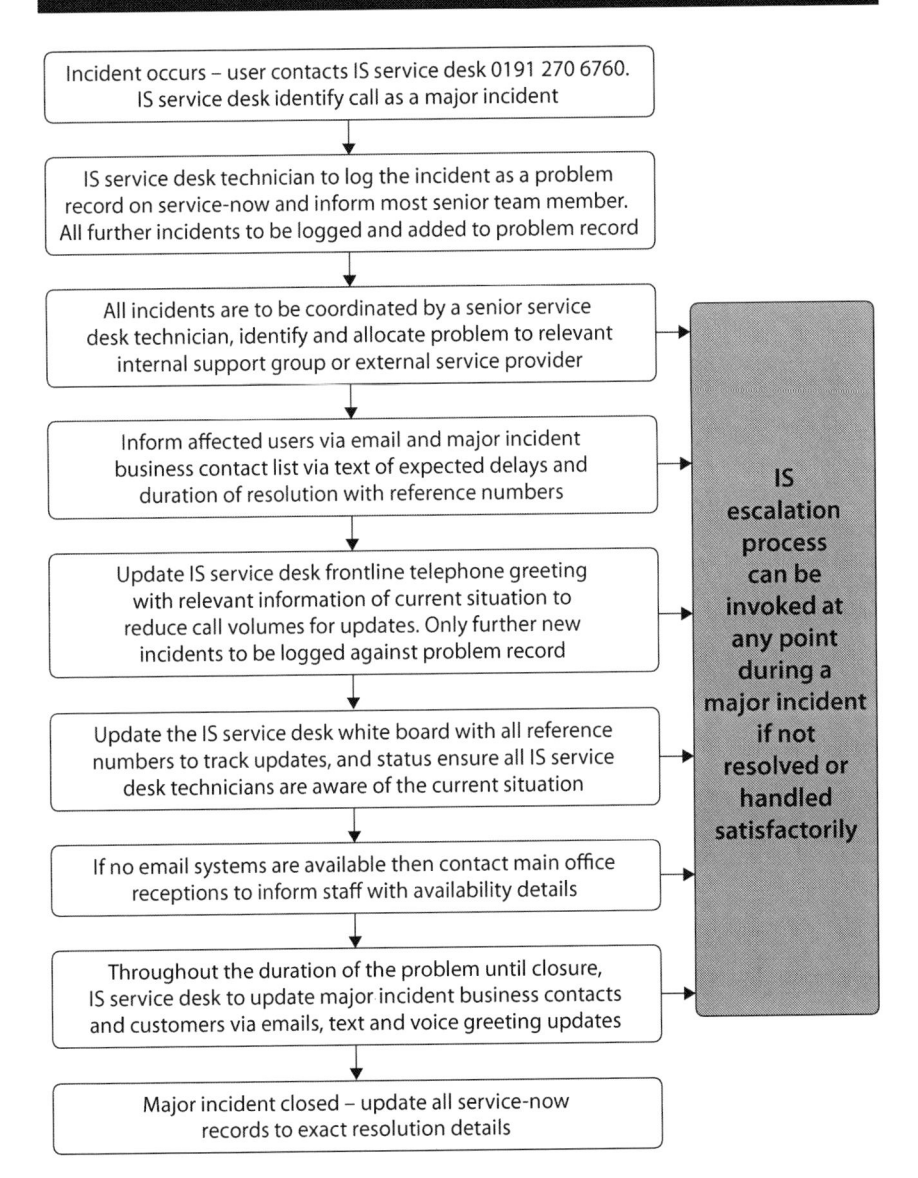

Incident occurs – user contacts IS service desk 0191 270 6760. IS service desk identify call as a major incident

↓

IS service desk technician to log the incident as a problem record on service-now and inform most senior team member. All further incidents to be logged and added to problem record

↓

All incidents are to be coordinated by a senior service desk technician, identify and allocate problem to relevant internal support group or external service provider →

↓

Inform affected users via email and major incident business contact list via text of expected delays and duration of resolution with reference numbers →

↓

Update IS service desk frontline telephone greeting with relevant information of current situation to reduce call volumes for updates. Only further new incidents to be logged against problem record →

↓

Update the IS service desk white board with all reference numbers to track updates, and status ensure all IS service desk technicians are aware of the current situation →

↓

If no email systems are available then contact main office receptions to inform staff with availability details →

↓

Throughout the duration of the problem until closure, IS service desk to update major incident business contacts and customers via emails, text and voice greeting updates →

↓

Major incident closed – update all service-now records to exact resolution details

IS escalation process can be invoked at any point during a major incident if not resolved or handled satisfactorily

Figure 13. Anchor Trust SDI award entry paper (2008).

Case study 11, regarding US internet service provider Clearwire, is exactly the type of issue you should be trying to avoid.

> **Case study 11: Clearwire**
>
> I stuck with Clearwire for 3 years, anticipating the new WiMax service. The signal was often weak and the speeds [slow], but it always worked. …Now that I have the new Clear service, my download speed has actually gotten slower! I'm averaging 1.2 Mbps… It started out at around 5 Mbps when I first hooked it up, but then it slowed down. I've talked with tech support a few times, but I'm told something different every time I call. Friday night the rep said that I had to agree to their terms of service to get my speed back. I agreed to that and the issue was supposed to be sent to their 'level 2' tech support for resolution. Two days later, it was no better, so I called back. They had no record of my earlier call and no trouble ticket had ever been created! The rep on my most recent call said he would let me speak to level 2 tech support, but in the end, it didn't happen. It never happens. Do they even have a level 2 tech support? Finally they agreed to send a technician out. That will happen in two days. 3 years ago, when I first got the service, they had to send a technician out and the guy basically said he couldn't help me and he left. Let's hope things go better this time.
>   I want this system to work, but the early results are dismal. And it's infuriating that their tech support people seem to just make stuff up to make you think they are really working on your problem. Call them 5 times, you'll get 5 different reasons and 'solutions', none of which work.
>
> (Karl Bode (2009), www.dslreports.com/shownews/Customers-Unhappy-With-Early-Clearwire-Launches-104511)

The failings are simple – such as the lack of a call record – and avoidable, but happen all too often, and there is a clear process shortfall that should have been addressed.

The five per cent of issues shown going to third-line support or beyond should be driven down to become only occasional as these represent very serious complaints, failings or costly problem issues.

Third-line customer service and support

Reaching this level – invariably a director, senior manager or expert in their specialist skill or product area – is to be avoided at all costs. Many organizations fail to address the fact that early resolution saves money, even if a complaint or customer may not be fully justified. Pret A Manger founder Sinclair Beecham told me at a seminar that he would much rather 'accept the customer's view and give away a sandwich or two to the small percentage of customers who have unjustified complaints' than spend hours of manager or administrative time on the issue. That may be harder to justify if you sell high-value goods or services, but even then it can sometimes be better to 'just move on' with a settlement that closes off an issue.

If you have reached this stage, then there are three words that spring immediately to mind: speed, action and cost. Already this issue has been through two tiers that have failed to find a resolution, and customer patience is being tested in addition to the rising cost to the organization. Speedy and decisive action at a reasonable cost must be the goal, bearing in mind the effect on both the customer and business in the future. Generally this can be achieved by, for example, a senior manager chairing a meeting to resolve the issue, involving all the relevant parties responsible, reaching an outcome, and not closing the meeting until this is achieved. There will be a few, only very exceptional, cases that cannot be resolved in this way.

Once the resolution is made it should be offered to the customer as a full and final solution, obviously leaving open the option for them of involving consumer law or following the complaint process. It is highly likely that, if the solution is reasonable and well presented to the customer this will be satisfactorily received.

Again, if your customer issue reaches this stage, you will really want to learn from it to avoid the expense and distraction of dealing with similar issues in the future. I recommend that third-line issues are reported at senior operational management or board level, together with their resolutions, remedial actions and improvements made as a result of the issue getting to this stage. This has the benefit of both alerting the leadership of the organization to the customer issues that might be damaging the business and of highlighting the improvements being made. As a result, you might identify further business opportunities or align with strategic plans being considered. This is additional to the 'back to the floor' tactic that should be undertaken periodically by all senior managers and directors to ensure they remain in touch with everyday customer concerns.

Dealing with complaints and compliments

Compliments and complaints can occur at any time, and both should be welcome. Even if they are unjustified, customer communications that give you feedback on what they think of your organization, products, services or people should always be encouraged as a key input to your service improvement process.

Compliments are obviously the most welcome, but it is often as difficult to use them effectively as it is to accept them, especially in a UK culture where it can be hard for us even to say 'thank you' when receiving good service. It is as important to receive and use compliments as it is to address complaints – the customer has made the effort to say something positive, and it would be both daft and ungracious not to use it. The first step is clearly acknowledging receipt, whether in person, on the telephone or in writing. It is an area where I believe few of us are highly skilled, and even in a social situation, most of us can find accepting compliments quite awkward. In general, a 'thanks' or 'that's kind of you' or 'we appreciate that great feedback' with a smile will suffice for person-to-person receipt. If it is a written compliment, then a short email or letter along similar lines is appropriate.

This is an unprecedented opportunity to learn more, and either at the time or shortly afterwards you should seek to gain more detail about what the customer found so positive that they felt moved to contact you with praise. We will examine the use of customer feedback and surveys in Chapter 7, but to use either effectively you should make every effort to qualify all feedback so that you are clear what customers are telling you.

Once you have captured the compliment, and there is no reason to capture it in a different way to a complaint or any other incident, it can be used in a number of ways. Traditionally this has tended to be in marketing the products or services about which the compliments were received, which is a sound use in supporting marketing initiatives to boost customer appeal. However, in recent years this has been overtaken in some organizations by 'customer rating' listings. These list both compliments and complaints and invite the customer to 'rate' the product or service and where used effectively have become a powerful tool for both the organization and the consumer. Good examples of this type of rating system can be found on the destination and hotel guidance site www.tripadvisor.com, the rating of purchased goods on Amazon and on the eBay marketplace, where the rating applies to the *transaction* experience and contributes to the trading record of both buyer and seller.

Consideration should be given to whether 'ratings' are right for your business or whether a simple use of compliments, either for marketing use or for staff motivation as in the following list, might apply. Customer First offered case study 12 as part of their 2009 Customer Service Week recognition, and there are several options from which to choose your method of using compliments.

> **Case study 12: Customer First: celebrating and recognizing great customer service**
>
> 1. Communicate customer service efforts internally – a service bulletin
> 2. Customer display board or area
> 3. Monthly theme day – pyjamas or home-made cakes
> 4. Cocktail invention afternoon – non alcoholic, named after team members
> 5. Forums – for recognition and promotion of service compliments
> 6. Rewards for those that go the extra mile
> 7. Staff nominations – Customer Service monthly champions
> 8. Regular get-togethers
> 9. Customer Review session – in regular team meetings
> 10. Customer compliments box
>
> (Lynsey Blackburn, Customer First UK, www.customerfirst.org/NewsArticle.aspx?newsid=175, September 2009)

Most of the suggestions are simply good opportunities to raise the profile of customer compliments and to recognize the staff members who have pleased customers. More importantly, they provide the opportunity to recognize the importance of customer service and positive feedback on a regular basis. Whichever you choose, it will make a positive contribution, but customer service forums, review meetings and bulletins include the people you need to involve very well, and the 'fun' events, such as the pyjama day, add a team-building dimension so these are the ones I would recommend.

Complaints are almost as welcome as compliments, and because they usually identify something that we can improve, perhaps they should actually be more welcome. The attitude to complaints has changed in recent years, particularly with the visibility in the media of customer dissatisfaction, with TV shows such as the BBC's 'Watchdog' and 'Rogue Traders'. This has led to a desire by most organizations not to be seen in programmes such as these or on other very public media such YouTube, Facebook and MySpace. One YouTube example that was very damaging to United Airlines in 2009 was the case of the country singer and musician, Dave Carroll, whose guitar was broken in transit. The poor United Airlines response and one year delay were featured for all to see in the form of a song that has had over 8 million hits. It is reputed to have lost United Airlines millions of dollars – 'within four days of the song going online, the gathering thunderclouds of bad PR caused United Airlines' stock price to suffer a mid-flight stall, and it plunged by 10 per cent, costing shareholders $180 million. Which, incidentally, would have bought Carroll more than 51,000 replacement guitars' (http://www.timesonline.co.uk/tol/comment/columnists/chris_ayres/article6722407.ece) – and is an ample demonstration of why you need to address complaints quickly and effectively.

There are many books on the subject of complaints; perhaps one of the best is *A Complaint is a Gift*, by Janelle Barlow and Claus Moller (1996). On the first page it states that 'No-one likes to receive complaints. Yet this is the method by which customers are to tell us how to run our business' so complaints are a vital part of customer feedback and shape how we deliver service to our customers in the future – we should worry if we are *not* receiving them.

Customers are able to access a significant amount of advice to help them complain, such as that from the UK government's consumer direct website.

Fortunately, there is an equivalent amount of advice available for organizations to guide their complaints handling process, such as the BS ISO 10002 standard *Guidelines for Complaints Handling in Organizations*. It supports my view, expressed in this book, on ensuring that complaints-handling data are available for top management review in subclause 5.3.3 and has extensive guidance on building the process framework, from setting in place a commitment and policy, to allocating responsibility and authority.

Every business needs to have a policy and system in place for receiving, handling, resolving and recording customer complaints. Clause 7 of BS ISO 10002 has guidance to show what you should do to advise the customer on the various routes to make a complaint and how the process will work, how to acknowledge, receive and track a complaint, and then how to progress it through assessment, investigation, response and closure. For example, subclause 7.2 lists the required information to acquire to ensure a customer's complaint can be handled effectively, such as the complaint description, what product or service is being complained about, the remedy required and the required completion date.

Throughout the complaint process there is no real difference in handling a complaint compared with any other request or enquiry – it may be resolved at tier one, two or three. The key difference is that the customer starts the process dissatisfied and may well be retained in the longer term by a good response to the complaint. The key to success here, as with other issues, is recognizing the value of a short-term fix and weighing that cost against further purchases by the customer – and their friends and family, whom they will tell if they have a bad experience. If you give your customer a good experience during the complaint process, as with my Virgin 'stranded in Florida' complaint in Chapter 2, you could ensure that the customer spends with you for life.

Summary

This chapter is probably the most difficult to read, and yet it is also the most important. It is difficult because processes are inherently dull, and it is important because process is the underlying bedrock that cements the success of great customer service people over the long term. Technology, which follows in Chapter 6, invariably will get more attention because it has features and interfaces, and you can put a box around it and say that you have invested perhaps £1m in the right choice of system, but unless you have the right processes alongside that technology, your £1m investment could well be wasted.

The customer service processes start and end with the customer. The three-tier recommendation helps you to look at the process from the customer inwards – rather than the customer being at the end of an inside-out process. But if you can prevent the customer contacting you by anticipating their every need or by having a product or service that never goes wrong so much the better. That is unlikely so when the customer contact occurs, handle and route it quickly and effectively to its resolution point – and remember it is much cheaper at the first point of contact: any delay or escalation will cost both you and the customer. Make it as easy as possible for the customer to contact you, by whatever means they wish.

Process is where standards can offer you huge value. I have referred to the guidance throughout in BS 8477 and BS ISO 10002 and from the SDI qualification standards, each of which will help you to check that you have covered comprehensively each process area. A standard I have not referred to until now is BS ISO/IEC 20000-2:2005 *Information technology – Service management –* Although this standard is intended for the management of IT service, it is the most comprehensive set of service standards available. In conjunction with this chapter, it can be used to enhance your customer service delivery to reach a new level. For example, it will offer guidance to help you to develop processes to manage change to the service environment, to develop your customer service catalogue, and to enhance service continuity and ongoing improvement. It was suggested in previous chapters that you look outside your own sector for guidance that can be applied – BS ISO/IEC 20000-2 is very relevant here.

Lastly, the customer service process offers a number of key learning opportunities that should not be missed by senior management. The leaders of the business should be involved in, and informed of, what is happening in the processes, especially in the failed areas and improvements on behalf of customers. This is the very future of their business, and it is crucial that they maintain full awareness of all the influencing factors.

Learning points

The most important points to remember are listed below.

- Understand the need to adopt a closed-loop process that starts and ends with the customer.
- Understand that if you can prevent the customer needing to contact you, it will save you time and money and help the customer get on with enjoying your product or service.
- If you cannot prevent issues, then fix them as close to the customer as possible as this will also save time and money.
- Use standards to ensure your processes cover every customer eventuality and ensure you support your first-line team as much as possible by providing clear guidelines for resolving customer issues and specifying the escalation route and appropriate next levels if you need to move issues up the chain.
- Inform your customer of how to contact you and what to expect if they have an issue.
- Maintain and review processes on a regular basis to ensure consistency and effectiveness, and use service processes as a constant source of learning about both your customer and your products and services.
- Consider the access requirements of disadvantaged customers and also any current consumer and business trading legislation that may affect your service.

The following is a short list of techniques and examples to consider and learn from.

Techniques:

- Use mystery shopping to look at your organization from the outside in – are you meeting the standard of customer service you have set or would wish to receive? Remember the 'moments of truth' specified in Chapter 1.
- Establish service level agreements and customer charters to define customer expectations in the same way that Chiltern District Council and Virgin Trains have done. You can go one step better and commit to specific response times for each type of customer contact route.
- Use the 'back to the floor' tactic to ensure the senior team are constantly aware of customer and frontline staff.
- Develop an appropriate system to exploit compliments and complaints to improve products and services further, and use the 'post-mortem' and senior manager-driven meetings to adopt a rapid and cost-effective action on larger outstanding customer issues to avoid extended cost and delay.

Examples:

- Sinclair Beecham's method at Pret A Manger was to invest in a customer complaint resolution early in the process to avoid extended time and cost to the business.
- Richer Sounds uses a customer service rating on their till receipt to give customer feedback on how well they were served, and this links to the staff reward system.
- Virgin Atlantic's post-mortem on our delayed flight back from Florida gathered all location and service staff and selected customers to learn from the events.

6

Customer service technology

Why it exists

Throughout this book, I have emphasized the importance of ensuring that the customer feels they are being dealt with in a human and personal way, even if the interaction is via technology, rather than face to face. In this chapter I will examine the various types of technology that are available to help you to deliver great service to your customers and the issues to be aware of when you are considering them. The emphasis here is 'help you to deliver'. As I have already stated, no technology can ever, in itself, form the full solution for customer service. Technology will always be dependent on human input and interaction to make it work effectively and will be closely aligned with the processes defined by your organization to deliver service to customers. Any technology you want should be able to help you deliver service better, faster and/or to more people.

The first point to consider is whether you actually need any form of customer service technology. If you are a small business you might just need a telephone with an automated answering service, a simple website and an email address, and a file or spreadsheet of customer contacts and data. This may be enough for the life of the business or, in a start-up situation, enough for the first year at least – you might not need to spend more until the business is well established and showing positive signs of growth. However, if the organization starts up at a reasonable size – say 10 people or more – and is projected to have hundreds of customers in its first year, customer service technology should be considered from day one. If not, business growth might be affected.

When you have decided that you do need some form of technology to help you deliver service to customers, what should that technology be and what criteria should you apply when selecting it? There are some basic questions that will help you to decide in any of the technology areas that we will cover:

Customer service technology   101

- Are our customers having trouble reaching us to get service of any sort?
- Are we offering the contact channels that our customers prefer to use, e.g. web chat, email, web self-service and mail order?
- Do we struggle to meet customer expectations of service? Does that relate to timeframe, knowledge or communication?
- Is our customer information complete, accurate and easily accessible?

These four questions should indicate where your issues lie and what technology you might need to help you solve it. The questions may also provide answers that will indicate a problem with your customer data, with a process or with the people involved. It is important to remember that the reason you are selecting customer service technology is to help your customers – the lifeblood of your organization – or to help you to manage them better. You are not selecting the latest gadgets or 'fun' features for your own use or pleasure as you would with your mobile phone or home entertainment system. Any features selected should add value either to customers or to your organization; it is surprising how often selections are governed by the 'wow' and not the 'how'. Technology selected on the basis of features alone invariably leads to it making a much smaller contribution than one selected using a rigorous project-based approach.

Michael Dell, in his book *Direct from Dell* (1999), which tells the story of how he grew Dell into one of the biggest PC suppliers in the world, said 'I founded the company with the intention of creating products and services based on a keen sense of a customer's input and the customer's needs'. Dell is famous for allowing its customers to 'design' their own system online with Dell then building them to order. This not only gives the customer the exact specification and support level they want, but also virtually eliminates the excess cost of buying and storing components that are not needed.

Dell puts all of the power in the hands of the customer, and that is what has made them successful. The transactions are almost always conducted online, making technology very much at the front of the front office in the business. Whatever technology you select, a customer does not want or need to understand the internal workings of your organization or any telephone and computer systems. They simply want to contact you and/or resolve their issue without having to repeat their details and information. When dealing with a larger business they expect you to have their file or data available; with a smaller business they expect you to know them personally. The lessons of Chapter 1 in knowing and understanding your customers apply, and a further consideration is that customers expect your technology to make them feel that they are dealing with one organization, whatever the location or method they contact you by. The implication is that whatever technology we apply, used by ourselves or by the customer, it needs to be customer friendly.

For example, I recently ordered a pair of shoes from the Clarks website. In addition to being a very customer friendly, easy-to-navigate site, it offered me the choice of having the shoes delivered to my home or collecting and paying for them at a local store. As my wife works 50 metres from a store I opted for that choice, and they sent me a text message and email three days later to say they were in the store. My wife was able to check they were the right shoes, pay for them, and I am now wearing them. It is not difficult to make it easy for customers to buy from you, but it is easy to make it hard. Make sure that your organization adopts the former approach when designing or selecting any technology.

The technology available and how to select it

Customer service operations today range from the simple face to face in a small shop or tradesperson business to vast, internationally spread contact centres where the customer could be contacting the organization thousands of miles away from where they live or made the purchase. Whatever the size of your business, the service principles throughout this book apply equally, but in this technology chapter the proportionate gain from the application of technology solutions is typically greater for larger organizations. For example, the linking of customer data and voice communications systems is unlikely to be of benefit to a two-person plumbing operation, but of significant benefit to a 500-employee business spread across several countries.

There is a vast array of tools aimed at helping customer service operations in all their forms, shapes and sizes. What this chapter will provide is a synopsis of each of the types of tool available, their general benefits and a view as to the likely usefulness of the tool type – from essential to marginal. There will also be some advice on which criteria to apply to select each tool. There is help available to guide your project to select the right technology, including the National Computing Centre's (NCC) Evaluation Centre service (www.evaluationcentre.com), which offers best practice guidance on the strategic and business requirements in addition to supplier evaluation, selection and product implementation. In addition, BS ISO/IEC 20000-2:2005, which I referred to in Chapter 5, has guidance on supplier selection and management of IT services and systems, in particular the application of SLAs and contract management to help with the supplier relationship, and the use of change, configuration and release management to minimize the risk of business impact from new or changed technology implementations. Clauses 7 (Relationship process) and 10 (Release process) are especially relevant.

Call Centre Focus magazine featured some recent research carried out by the Customer Experience Foundation (CEF) in conjunction with Empirix, which showed the danger of customer technology projects that were not managed well:

> Project overruns incurred when rolling out new call centre technology typically add 90 per cent to the original project budget costs. More than half of the [100] respondents said that, in addition to cost overruns, delays had had a negative impact on more than half their calls.
>
> Among the largest group of projects examined, with projected budgets of between £1.1 million and £3 million, the average cost overruns amounted to between £1 million and £2.7 million on top of original budgets. In addition to the overspend, the survey also discovered that the typical delay to a project was over seven months. The most severely delayed projects involved delivering databases, CTI, CRM, IVRs and ACDs.
>
> (*Call Centre Focus*, September 2009)

The message here is clear: spend sufficient time planning your project to select and implement your technology and ensure that it matches the needs of both the customer and the business. Seek advice too on the delivery method for any solution you choose: Software as a Service (SaaS) and 'cloud computing' offer services that you can use straight from the vendor's web-hosted site; you may well not want to buy and install your own version of software.

Contact centres

Although contact centres are not technologies as such, they typically act as the owner and repository for customer service technology. A contact centre could be as small as a five-person customer service or sales team or as big as thousands of staff across the world linked by technology solutions. A contact centre aims to handle the majority of customer interactions. It safeguards the company's reputation and long-term customer loyalty and tries to avoid giving customers a bad experience, for example long wait times if they call on the telephone. *Marketing* magazine recently asked contact centre experts for their view on some of the common contact centre problems that they had identified, such as long call waiting times. The response below was typical:

> *Rachel Robinson*, divisional managing director, Teleperformance [contact centre provider]: Nobody should be expected to wait 30 minutes – technology exists today to prevent this. Call-query technology can be employed in such a way as to recognise that people are holding and offer options during their wait time. For example, give them the option to leave their details for a call back. (Abbot, 2009)

The best contact centres are now generally adept at preventing call queues that lead to delays such as the one above, and most employ a mix of technology that contains customer and product or service data linked to the communication systems being used – voice, text, chat or email. The customer data is generally collected and stored on a customer relationship management (CRM) system, which is the first of the technologies that we will examine.

Customer relationship management systems

CRM systems are principally designed to capture and store customer information for use in the effective management of the relationship with customers. The resulting database of customer details, perhaps covering name, address, contact information, and purchase and service history (as a minimum), can then be used for a variety of customer-related purposes, as shown in Figure 14.

Many of the range of purposes are basic functions that any organization will need to carry out. That is why some form of CRM system – once a business grows to a reasonable size – becomes an essential piece of technology to implement. The definition of size will vary by the type of business, but the criteria in the chapter introduction will guide you, such as: Are our customers having trouble reaching us to get service of any sort? Are we offering the contact channels that our customers prefer to use? Do we struggle to meet customer expectations of service? Does that relate to timeframe, knowledge or communication? Is our customer information complete and easily accessible? You can see how a CRM system could help address some of these issues and then be used for more advanced functions. This might include using customer data and purchasing history to improve product quality or to conduct a sales and marketing campaign to a particular group of customers. A CRM system can be really beneficial to an organization wishing to manage its customer interactions and relationships. Many organizations use these types of system across the business so that all staff are aware of what a particular customer's history is at any given time, which allows every department to 'think customer' whatever their role. The supplier of one of these systems, Oracle, carried out research among its European customers which illustrated the impact of CRM on their businesses.

Figure 14. Customer relationship management.

Case study 13

According to the research, a key objective for customer service managers is to keep the customer happy. In fact, contact centre managers prioritized operational objectives in the following order:

1. 83% of European contact centre managers viewed dealing with customers to their satisfaction as highly important
2. 66% of European contact centre managers viewed keeping customers for as little time as possible in call queues as highly important

> 3. Interestingly, objectives governing operational efficiency, such as the number of calls dealt with per hour or minimizing staff numbers, were low on the list of priorities.
>
> [In addition, the Oracle survey noted that] consumers' principle complaints include:
>
> 1. Having to endure long call queues (77%)
> 2. Having to repeat their query each time they speak to someone new (75%)
> 3. Being passed between too many departments (55%)
> 4. Customer service representatives not understanding their employer's business (43%)
> 5. Receiving inconsistent answers each time (43%).
>
> Worryingly, 43% of contact centre managers maintain that customers never have to repeat their query – which just goes to highlight the disconnect between the aspirations for service delivery and the reality experienced by the European public.
>
> When customers were specifically asked what were the main drivers of a dissatisfactory service, 43% of respondents identified ineffective customer service staff.
>
> Yet contact centre managers claim that staff are being let down by inadequate tools, training and processes. When questioned as to what would most improve the level of customer service within the organization, contact centre managers identified the following measures:
>
> 1. Providing customer-facing staff with better quality information (58%)
> 2. Improved customer service procedures (45%)
> 3. Effective call routing (44%)
> 4. Empowering staff with more responsibility to make decisions (38%)
> 5. Advising callers, while they are waiting, of alternative ways of resolving their queries (for instance, email and the internet). (Oracle, 2008)

The report also showed that companies could decrease contact centre costs by driving the top 20 frequently asked questions to lower-cost channels such as the internet and by intelligently prioritizing and re-routing customer interactions to the appropriate channel during busy periods, thereby alleviating long call queues for customers. There are further ongoing business benefits that could accrue from implementing CRM systems – understanding customer purchase behaviour better, identifying the most profitable customers, cross-selling other products, and adopting a more personal and targeted approach to marketing. This should lead not only to more sales, but also to improved customer satisfaction and loyalty through more regular and specific contact.

Internet-based systems for CRM are available and can be accessed for a monthly or annual fee (SaaS). They can also be bought conventionally off the shelf and implemented in-house or tailored to specific requirements by consultants and software engineers. As with any such purchase, the more you want in terms of specific tailored functionality, the more staff you want to access the system, and the more connectivity with other technology you want, the more you will spend. CRM systems can cost from the low thousands to millions of pounds. When choosing a CRM system, you may wish to consider how you record and track complaints. Separate specialist complaints management software is available, but you could also integrate complaints into your CRM system. In either case you will need to ensure that you are able to create the correct documentation trail to resolve customer complaints.

Implementation in line with your customer service model and process requirements is essential, and at every project stage you should look at the system from a customer's perspective. Will it be customer friendly and add value? Will appropriate customers and staff members be told about how they will be trained to use the system? Will customer data be secure and accessible by the right people? Will you be able to carry out all the analysis and segmentation tasks that you want to? All of these issues and others that are important to your business must be addressed or you risk not getting as much from your system as you would want. Typical failure areas for implementation projects can include inadequate definition of requirements, poor leadership, a lack of commitment from staff or management and/or a lack of communication. Using advice from the NCC's evaluation centre service or guidance from BS ISO/IEC 20000 is desirable and can help to avoid these and the potential extra cost.

Telephony and voice communications

This section would previously have contained a very limited range of simple telephones, recording devices and exchanges. Today there is a vast choice of technology to handle voice-based communication. The ability to link this to the customer data stored on a CRM system has proved a powerful combination, which allows first-line customer staff to access both voice functionality and customer data from one screen. This has been successful in enhancing most customer interactions – some of the telephony tools involved are listed here. Most will have volume-handling or cost-saving potential for larger contact centres, but for the smaller organization, the CTI (computer telephony integration) and IVR (interactive voice response) technology will be beneficial for handling first-line customer interactions and their follow-up, usually in conjunction with a CRM type system.

- *Computer telephony integration (CTI).* CTI is, as the name implies, what is used for linking the CRM system with the voice technology. CTI has the potential to offer a wide range of benefits to a customer service operation, basically to streamline and improve the efficiency of customer interactions. It offers agents on-screen phone control and the integration of email, voicemail, web and fax contacts. It also provides features such as caller identification and screen population, which draws from the CRM database to populate the screen with relevant information about the caller. Depending on this outcome the caller can then be routed to the staff with the right skills or knowledge to help.
- *Interactive voice response (IVR).* The integration of CTI and IVR is essential if an organization is to harness the full potential of both technologies. IVR has the ability to detect (speech recognition) and to interact with customer voice messages and to handle simple details without human interaction. It can prevent customers from having to repeat information when transferred to another agent therefore improving the productivity and efficiency of agents' time and improving customer service. It also helps to handle high call volumes and to reduce overall customer handling expense. Voice automation needs to be handled with care, however, as many callers can get frustrated and refuse to 'speak to a machine'. It may be that you use this technology to segment out customers with premium or specific service needs, which offers you the ability to offer different levels of service.
- *Voice over Internet Protocol (VoIP).* VoIP is a communication method for voice over the internet or other switching network. It is commonly used to facilitate any voice communication at a cost-effective price, and perhaps the best-known consumer brand is Skype. It offers significant savings over conventional telephony and is now in wide use. VoIP has been associated with poor sound quality, distortion and lag. However, as technology has advanced these issues have been overcome and the sound quality is now as good as a conventional landline, and internet connection is becoming increasingly stable. Another benefit of VoIP, which is especially important in customer service organizations, is the quality and ease with which calls can be recorded.
- *Speech recording.* Speech recording is now widely used to record calls for training of staff in how to handle customer interactions better, to verify compliance

issues, to form records of calls for dispute or legal reasons, and generally to form a log of interactions. It is especially useful for one-to-one staff coaching purposes, giving a supervisor the ability to point out good and bad in the way a customer was dealt with for future improvements.
- *Speech recognition and analytics.* Some of us will have experienced speech recognition applications if we have called our bank or credit card company and spoken our date of birth or account number into the telephone receiver. It is often integrated into an IVR system to help capture customer details without the customer needing to speak to a staff member. Speech analytics is currently emerging as a way to make more use of speech interaction with customers, in order to boost productivity, reduce contact centre costs and improve the customer experience. It works by analysing call content, flow and customer emotion to see whether there are trends or unrecognized opportunities. Analytics is not yet mature, but with the constant drive to reduce costs while improving productivity and service levels, it will become a mainstream tool in the next few years.

Self-service

The provision of a (typically web-based) customer self-help facility has become commonplace in today's service environment. These facilities have been championed as an effective method for reducing the number of calls directed to first-line customer service regarding common, basic problems and providing immediate 'service' from any location at any time. Oracle published a white paper which shows the potential cost saving:

> For simple inquiries, such as address and phone number changes, self-service deflects a significant number of contact center calls to the Web, which is much more efficient. By improving their systems and adding essential content, companies can reduce their call volumes by 20 percent or more ... Research has shown that average call center costs are $5.50 per call, but some can be as high as $50 per contact. In contrast, a conservative estimate of the average cost per Web self-service transaction is $0.10. Also, sending bills costs $0.44 online versus $1.10 for a paper bill. Even in small call centers annual self-service savings quickly shoot past the six-figure mark and many enterprises can realize cost reductions in the multimillions. (Oracle, 2009)

This extract is one of many such articles and case studies that report that a significant number of calls or emails that would previously have been directed to first-line support can be consistently deflected to an online self-help resource. These can involve interactive dialogue with customers, or simply a list of FAQs. There are good levels of customer acceptance today, which is an essential feature of a successful self-help facility. The time taken to achieve a consistent level of deflected calls and the proportion of calls that an organization might aim to deflect depends on the individual situation in each operation. Variables include the technical ability and confidence of customers; the technical level of information included in the self-help facility; and awareness of the facility and how acceptable it will be to the established culture. Existing processes will impact the time it takes for the facility to be truly established and deemed 'successful' or otherwise; however, figures show that it is widely accepted.

Research undertaken by the Bright Index (2009), the UK and Scandinavian contact centre performance measurement specialist, revealed that there was a correlation between the provision of self-service and highly satisfied customers with the average self-service level now being over 40 per cent (and in the banking sector as high as 70 per cent). 'We see that the top performing centres have a high percentage of self service calls. Customers like self service when it's set up correctly and there is the option to speak to a live agent. We however saw a worrying trend increase of 16% to 22% of abandoned calls in self service from 2007 to 2008 indicating that consumers are growing tired of poor scripts' (Rennstam and Jacobs, 2009).

In everyday life there are many examples of self-service. Most banks have internet-based banking services and have excellent, easy to understand websites that allow you to carry out your banking transactions from your home or laptop computers. We have long used airline, hotel or car hire websites to book flights or holidays. The experience with the Clarks shoes website mentioned earlier in the chapter was a positive example of self-service with good website performance for my 'first time' in terms of ease of navigation and order process, then follow up using text, email and their store network to actually receive the goods. The Ryanair website, however, still overloads customers with confusing pop-ups and the need to confirm that you have read their terms and conditions more than once – and all before you get the total price of travel.

Self-service, implemented and marketed well, is a really powerful tool for handling large volumes of customer interactions and can create a positive boost to customer satisfaction. It is important to understand the primary use of the facility; is it mainly an alternative means of purchasing your products or services, or mainly to help fix problems with them? It is important that the information on the self-service portal is accurate and consistently maintained so that it meets the needs of customers in either case, as if the customer experience is poor or the facility is not designed or marketed well, it can fail to deliver a return on an often significant investment – in addition to impacting on customer loyalty levels.

Self-service and self-help require product and process knowledge to help customers – and staff – to direct and resolve interactions quickly. The specialist KM Consortium for Service Innovation (www.serviceinnovation.org), which includes Microsoft, HP and Novell as members, summarizes the types of demand we have identified below, and introduces the knowledge concept, whether it be provided by the first-line staff, the organization or the customer community. The types of demand and their respective support paths, typically generated by 'customer exceptions', its definition of customer issues, are:

1. assisted support, where customers want to talk to the vendor and submit their issue through contact by phone, email or chat;
2. self-service, where customers use automated service tools that deliver help integrated into the product or website;
3. communities, where customers want to interact with other customers and ask questions, respond or vote on the issues of others, rate services and comment via online forums or blogs.

Knowledge management

Providing effective and useful knowledge to help customer service staff give better service to customers through knowledge management (KM) systems is often perceived as being time consuming and expensive. However, when practised effectively, with information made readily accessible, huge improvements in service delivery and performance can be achieved. The Consortium for Service Innovation suggests that several improvements in performance of various customer service functions are possible with effective KM, including improved call resolution time, higher first-level 'fix' rates, faster staff knowledge acquisition, higher call deflection rates and general call reduction due to the root cause of issues being addressed better.

A good KM system should provide staff with easily accessible, relevant knowledge. Advances in knowledgebase technology have improved the speed and accuracy of data retrieval. Systems are now available that have the ability to work using association, i.e. mimicking the way in which the human brain solves problems and issues. The best technologies associate information and data with 'experiences' that can be related to typical customer service cases. The relevant data can therefore be retrieved extremely quickly as the system will intuitively link questions to answers and make assumptions, for example that the answer to one issue may well solve a similar issue. The technology also 'learns' from previous successful experiences and so becomes more accurate and more attuned to its particular environment with use. This in turn improves the accuracy of knowledge retrieval, both from the agent and customer perspective. In addition, combining technology with a best practice method called Knowledge Centred Support (KCS), developed by the Consortium for Service Innovation, offers all service functions a clearly defined set of practices to capture simple and easily meaningful, reusable knowledge while providing a vastly improved level of support.

Given its relative ease of deployment, there is a significant opportunity for larger organizations to gain an important competitive advantage through KM. It will take commitment to ensure that staff and managers adopt the new practices, and continual updating of knowledge 'items', but the payback can be excellent.

Post and email management

If customers send you a letter today, it is typically more time-consuming than other methods of contact. Larger organizations often scan physical letters into an electronic form to make internal distribution easier and quicker. This is generally cost-effective and cuts out the physical mail delivery cost. The response to the customer should, of course, remain in letter form. When customers send you an email they expect to receive a quick and relevant response in line with your SLA commitment. If they do not, they are likely to phone or email again, which increases customer frustration and the workload in your contact centre.

If you introduce email management software, which can integrate with your other systems, it will usually automatically acknowledge receipt of a customer email and will sometimes detect and answer the customer issue with a pre-programmed automatic response. You could expect to reduce repeat emails by around 25 per cent and trim email handling time by around half. Both post and email systems, especially for larger organizations, are highly useful in handling these forms of customer interaction, especially in integrating them with other forms of contact to form a complete customer record. The organization can either assign dedicated staff to email response – or can make it part of a general role for service-facing staff. This will also be a choice for the following chat technology.

Chat and associated services

Customers accessing service via a self-help facility can be supported by chat or instant messaging facilities. There is also a fast growing population of internet users who are accustomed to interacting in this way via chat rooms and Skype, and who do not want to pick up the phone or wait for an answer to an email. Chat will be a first choice – or can provide a convenient 'back up' for all customers using self-help – and customers can contact staff in real time via chat if they become stuck using web-based services.

An independent Forrester Research, Inc. report from 2008 showed ways to calculate good ROI of chat, and also highlighted the reasons customers liked to use chat services (Figure 15).

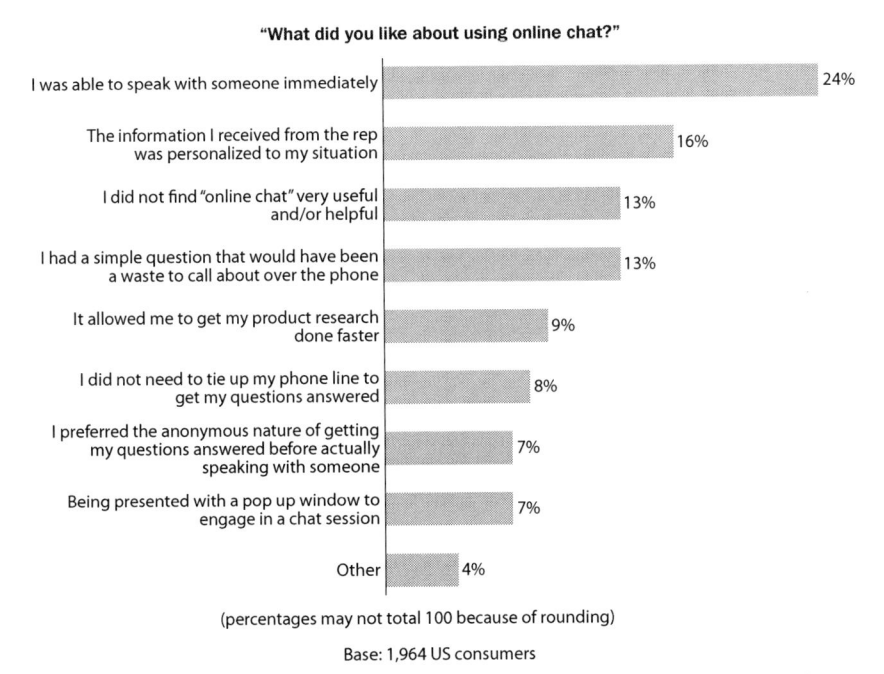

"What did you like about using online chat?"

Response	%
I was able to speak with someone immediately	24%
The information I received from the rep was personalized to my situation	16%
I did not find "online chat" very useful and/or helpful	13%
I had a simple question that would have been a waste to call about over the phone	13%
It allowed me to get my product research done faster	9%
I did not need to tie up my phone line to get my questions answered	8%
I preferred the anonymous nature of getting my questions answered before actually speaking with someone	7%
Being presented with a pop up window to engage in a chat session	7%
Other	4%

(percentages may not total 100 because of rounding)

Base: 1,964 US consumers

Source: North American Technographics® Retail, Marketing, Customer Experience, And Service Benchmark Survey, Q4 2007

Figure 15. Chat solves a broad spectrum of customer needs (Forrester Research Inc., 2008).

Messaging technologies such as e-chat or live chat can also be used to increase the productivity of customer service staff. They are able to deal with an increased workload when using this medium. It can enable staff to manage around twice the number of sessions they would otherwise have been able to when taking a telephone call. Messaging is a good tool for managing and communicating with customers effectively and efficiently and has usually created very good customer feedback. Some organizations have taken the technology a step further, especially in the online gaming environment, but also in other sectors. They are using 'avatars', otherwise known as digitized virtual assistants, to act as online customer service staff who will 'chat' with customers through an image visible on their computer screen. Chat is an excellent way of interacting with customers and can achieve very rapid returns on investment, even for smaller organizations. It will typically help to increase first-line fixes, assist customers 'instantly' and reduce the incidence of customers leaving your website without completing their transaction. It should therefore be considered as a core technology to use.

Web 2.0 and social media

Web 2.0 really refers to the latest ways we use the internet and is not a 'technology' as such. Where it applies to delivering customer service is in being aware of how your customers want to interact with you on the internet. Video game manufacturer Ubisoft is a good example, found in *Customer Strategy* magazine (2009):

> Ubisoft's customers tend to be young, web savvy people who are comfortable multi-tasking and searching for solutions from a range of sources: forums, social media such as Facebook or Twitter and supplier websites. Web 2.0 is a very loosely defined term, but if you are looking for an illustration of what a typical next-generation internet user would look like, this is it. This involves understanding your customer (in particular the 'generational' aspect) and tailoring a service that best suits. (West, 2009)

In the same issue, *Customer Strategy* interviewed Andy Barker, director of consumer services for Sony Computer Entertainment, in an article called 'Player number one has entered the game...' about the rise of email contacts and the use of SaaS. One major change, according to Baker, is that the culture of customer contact has changed in recent years. 'Email traffic has doubled over the last two years. Whereas once customers readily made a call, the same is now true with email' (Customer Strategy, 2009). As well as email, Sony Playstation customers are increasingly comfortable using the web for support. 'A lot of people choose self-help now ... for those who don't find what they are looking for, they default to email. People are prepared to spend longer now looking on-line for answers' (Customer Strategy, 2009).

My experience is that although Web 2.0 will continue to be an effective delivery mechanism for customer service applications, the use of social media and community-based networks for service is very much in its infancy and should mostly be avoided for the delivery of everyday, mainstream customer service – at least for the time being. Community-based networks are already here, however, and do offer the opportunity to gain valid and fresh customer feedback on your products and services, hence organizations should take control of this media to avoid being forced to react to the community that is building up around them. Online reviews and forums are now one of the first ports of call for customers seeking advice from others who are willing to share their experience. (See Chapter 7 for further guidance.) The word 'social' sums up the warning signs for most social media – the use of these applications for business is inconsistent and currently unproven. Many people will not even have come across wikis, mashups, crowd sourcing and widgets, which relate to website pages, applications and community solutions.

According to Ann Marcus from the Consortium for Service Innovation (2006), a website 'should have the ability to provide content that is filtered by the context, environment, critical variables and experience of the intended audience'. It should have up-to-date knowledge feeds to ensure that the latest solutions are always available, and customers should have multiple ways to access content, for example top 10 FAQs by product area, table of contents look-up, search tool and bookmarks. There should be no 'dead ends': if a customer does not find helpful information, they should have the option to request assisted support, via a feature such as click to call, click to chat and click to submit an incident. The customer's 'website experience – the click stream and search strings – should be captured so that the support person they connect with can grasp the issues and context and get more quickly engaged in finding a solution' (Marcus, 2006).

This is an area that will see rapid development over the next few years, so it is worth watching for the emergence of a consistent and reliable customer service tool that could add value for your organization. It will require significant research and development efforts by both vendors and service organizations to reach that stage.

Mobile and remote support

With the increasing trend for home and mobile working, many organizations need to consider how to support both staff and customers who do this. This has led to a proliferation of support options, especially for the technology products involved in enabling mobile and home working. Some of these relate to a particular brand or organization's range of products, for example Apple's 'MobileMe' service that allows you to sync and support all of your Apple devices such as your iPhone and Mac PC through one online service. It also offers 'Genius Bars' (where you can pop into their stores and have an Apple specialist answer your query), free in-store workshops where they show you how to use various devices and applications, and you can purchase one-to-one packages that provide you with an opportunity to book training on specific products or applications as and when you need it.

Other services support a range of products sold such as the 'Geek Squad' service from Carphone Warehouse, which is available for any technology bought from their store or website and is also available by independent subscription. This service will help with most technology issues and offers a value-added option to the purchase of the product. All of these types of service place a heavy reliance on their ability to 'dial in' to the product in question through remote support software (RSS). This allows them to fix many problems without physically needing to see or touch the device and gives them the ability to 'coach' the customer on how to get round this problem next time.

If sales or support of technology is your business, this remote support software is essential and has a very rapid return on investment. In fact the business model is unsustainable without it – if you had to visit the customer or insist they come into the shop, the cost and convenience mix would be unattractive. There is the security issue to consider, especially if you are supporting customers from an overseas location. Most organizations now integrate a security 'sign off' for customers for each transaction so that they are clear when the support team is accessing their device. Remote support can also be helped by the use of simulations of customer work patterns or device images.

The prevalence of mobile messaging will increase significantly over the next few years, with more and more applications moving to mobile devices. (The Apple iPhone is a prime example.) Mobile users now have access to communication channels 24/7 and service providers will be expected to provide ever-increasing levels of availability and access to support/customer service. This will need to be borne in mind as it will inevitably place pressure on all customer service providers to deliver more and more 'instant support'. Amazon raised the bar on internet-based service and the new mobile technology players will do the same for mobile support.

Summary

We need technology to help us with customer service as soon as we start to build our business beyond a few people and customers. It will help us to deliver better, faster and to more people if we make the right choices and implement them well to complement our selected processes and people. A sale transaction hopefully will be only the start of a customer's interaction with you. Before you decide what you will buy, consider the issues your customers are potentially struggling with in reaching you or getting a response from you in good time alongside the question of whether you are responding in a cost-effective way. Is it technology that will make the difference, or is there a flaw in your people or processes?

For each type of technology that you have identified, what are the benefits and drawbacks for your business for each of them? The benefits should include shared and accessible data, better service and customer satisfaction at a reduced cost, and retained and loyal customers. There are potential drawbacks to consider and balance, such as poor business and customer alignment and lack of flexibility, the cost of training and roll-out, and the need for buy-in and commitment from all teams.

It will be a demanding time to research, select and implement whatever you want and you will be subjected to buying pressure from vendor organizations. You might be well served by seeking the help of expert consultants or the NCC's Evaluation Service if you do not have experience of the area you are considering. BS ISO/IEC 20000-2 has guidance on supplier selection and the management of change and release of systems across businesses that you should build into your thinking. Some vendors will allow you to evaluate the technology, or run a pilot system before you buy. When these options are available, invest the time and resources to test-drive the system in your environment, against your service model, before you purchase.

There are many impressive features available when you are evaluating your potential selections, and not all of the technologies and features will be appropriate for customer service at your organization. Established tools such as self-service and help, email management and chat will deliver sound benefits if implemented and marketed well, but the return on investment for some of the new social media options is not tested. If you are prepared to experiment and be at the leading edge then that is fine, but on no account should you continue if service is being adversely affected.

Customer service is a crucial area for the long-term health of your business, and the tools you select will cost a significant amount of money. You need to be sure you make the right choices.

Learning points

- Understand that there should be clear business reasons for the selection, purchase and implementation of your customer service technology. Do you really need the technology you are considering? Will it help you provide service better, faster and/or to more people?
- Consider and define precisely the customer service issue, problem or improvement that you are addressing and remain clearly focused on it.
- Projects often stagnate or collapse because of a failure to identify quick wins that can be achieved in the early phase of implementation. To capture management attention, secure support for subsequent phases and maintain momentum; it is vital that you define those quick wins and communicate your achievements as soon as they are realized.
- Seeking assistance from experts if you do not have them in-house will save you time and money and will help you to avoid common mistakes in the selection, purchase and implementation process.
- Customer-friendly technology is essential in all systems that customers interact with – whether an IVR telephone system, an ATM or an internet interaction. You should also ensure that your other systems present no customer service barriers.
- Top performing contact centres use proven technology, such as self-service and chat, to help them handle high volumes of interactions cost effectively with good levels of customer satisfaction. As your customer service volumes grow you will need to consider technology to keep service costs competitive.
- Knowledge to help resolve customer issues will be found across your organization. You should identify the sources and capture as much as you can to underpin the self-service and first-line interactions to achieve better, faster answers.

The following is a short list of techniques and examples to consider and learn from.

Techniques:

- To ensure success of both selection and implementation, the involvement of both staff and customers through a focus group to test practicality and customer friendliness is essential and commonly used to good effect. The new Windows 7 from Microsoft has made a strength of this and advertises customer involvement heavily.
- The use of the relationship process in BS ISO/IEC 20000-2, clause 7, will give you more control over the management of the supplier relationship and covers key areas such as contract management, where you will need to assign a manager

- to take responsibility, and service reviews, where your provider should plan and record meetings and follow-up as agreed.
- The use of an independent expert or service such as in the NCC's Evaluation Centre will help to ensure that your project is planned and executed to industry best practice and help budgets and timelines to stay on track.
- Apple's 'MobileMe' service has developed and enhanced the customer experience and brand loyalty by integrating support and synchronization of devices that many customers would be using, such as Mac computers and iPhones. They find it very convenient to be supported under one easily accessible internet-based umbrella and are typically buying more Apple products to get the support offered.
- Whatever technology you get, the use of it across the organization – and how it interfaces with different teams and customers – should be marketed well so that awareness, buy-in and usage are high. Customers should also be made aware of any new interaction methods or possibilities.
- The best use of first-line telephony should be regularly recorded and tested, possibly using mystery shoppers, and used to ensure continual improvement and consistency.
- For knowledge systems to work well and stay current, know-how 'champions' that will encourage and proliferate usage will help to ensure knowledge stays valid.

Examples:

- Give your customer control of their product and service, as Dell has done.
- The Carphone Warehouse Geek Squad service has added a valuable option to a customer purchase of goods.
- The Clarks shoe website offers customers a good purchase experience in conjunction with email and text communication. Allowing customers to 'try before you buy' in their store chain is also a good way to engage customers better.
- Avoid having a complex website, such as Ryanair's, as you run the risk of customers abandoning transactions in frustration.

7

Measurement of customer service success

Goals to determine success or failure

In this book I have identified what is important in order to achieve great customer service, but, as any CEO will tell you, it is the results that count. Results are the most important aspect for both organizations and customers, and they are what we are most often judged by. For a CEO the success of the business will ultimately be judged by the delivery of regular profits and sustained growth over a number of years. For a not-for-profit organization, success indicators will be based around the quality of the product or service delivered – and whether it is at a reasonable cost. In customer service we also need to know whether we are successful – or whether we are failing. I have already suggested that closed-loop processes are important to ensure that you achieve a result and 'closure' for customers, and this chapter closes the customer service loop that started in Chapter 1 with the first task, that of understanding our customers. Such is the power and speed of circulation of customer feedback today that business success or failure can be dramatically impacted by it. The United Airlines YouTube video by Dave Carroll mentioned in Chapter 5 is a case in point. On a more positive note, Microsoft, whose release of Windows 7 we highlighted for 'customer friendliness' in Chapter 6, has clearly learned from the poor customer feedback on its Vista product and has made a marketing virtue of involving their customers in the design of Windows 7.

It is important for customer service managers to 'establish a process for performance monitoring, evaluation and reporting of customer service' (BS 8477). The standard goes on to give guidance in clause 6, where it recommends that 'feedback relating to customer service should be obtained from sources including: customers; employees; regular management checks/monitoring; audits; complaints and any other redress mechanisms, including ombudsmen' (2007). The key source of course is customers, and the standard goes on to recommend how their feedback might be gathered – through, for example, focus groups and satisfaction surveys. The draft ISO standard ISO/TS 10004 *Quality management – Customer satisfaction – Guidelines for monitoring and measuring* is due for publication in 2010 and offers additional guidance, especially in the area of using surveys to measure customer satisfaction. It will assist in deciding how to identify the right customers to choose and how to assess their expectations. It will also show you how to collect customer satisfaction data and how to analyse and report on the results.

Before establishing what measures or metrics are best for determining how successful you are, it is important to understand what your goals are from the measurement and reporting process. To help you to set your own organization's goals, I believe that the main reasons for measuring customer service success are:

- Brand credibility: Is your brand reputation being improved or damaged by the customer's experience with you?
- Customer service status and credibility: Is service and the team involved in delivering it given enough priority and attention in your organization?
- Customer retention and loyalty reinforcement: Is the service experience helping to keep customers over a long period?
- Revenue improvement and loss reduction: Is service helping to boost direct or follow-on sales or to reduce returns and refunds?
- Business improvement/savings and innovations: Is the service process helping to identify product or process improvements and/or innovations?

These reasons should form a sound basis for your goals. Most of the items on this list have already featured in this book, but the second item in particular is worth reinforcing at this stage as it is fundamental to ensure that the customer service team is recognized as a crucial contributor to overall business success. You may recall that, in Chapter 3, I suggested some success indicators of my own that could be adopted as underlying customer service and business principles: Are you still in business where some competitors are not? Are your sales levels competitive in your marketplace? Do you regularly see returning customers and attract customers by the recommendation of others? Do people seem to like your organization and talk about it in good terms, often thanking you for the things you do for them? These principles will underpin all of the measures that appear in this chapter.

Before we go on to look at which measures will best serve your purpose, it is worth stating that, even if you do establish and report on the best customer and business measures, you will always find people who do not believe what you are telling them. The loss of trust in public figures has led to a general distrust of any facts that do not correspond to the reader's views or experiences. For example, a July 2009 UK Customer Satisfaction Index (UKCSI is a measure of national customer satisfaction in the UK) presented by the Institute of Customer Service had interviewed 25,000 UK adults and concluded that companies were focusing on their customers and not on cost cutting in the economic downturn. This was reported to have helped to continue the upward trend of the quality of UK customer satisfaction, and 46 per cent of the respondents thought that UK customer service was the best in the world. This UKCSI report, of course, provoked comment from respected commentators across the world, including *Forbes* magazine in the USA. Josie Richardson wrote in the 10 July online article 'Are you being served?': 'Just as you thought customer service in Britain couldn't get any worse, a new poll claims that British service is the best in the world. Well, according to the Brits, at least' (Forbes.com, July 2009). Tourism and food retail were the top-performing sectors in the UKCSI chart (Figure 16).

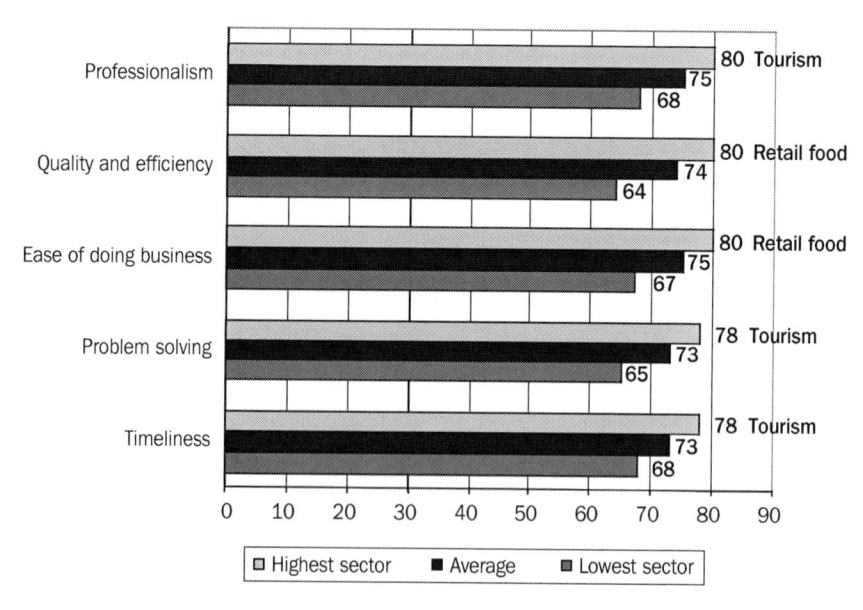

Category	Highest sector	Average	Lowest sector
Professionalism	80 Tourism	75	68
Quality and efficiency	80 Retail food	74	64
Ease of doing business	80 Retail food	75	67
Problem solving	78 Tourism	73	65
Timeliness	78 Tourism	73	68

Figure 16. UKCSI survey, July 2009, http://ukcsi.com/Latestresults.aspx (website image is reproduced by permission of the Institute of Customer Service).

Richardson's article went on to quote foreign nationals living in London who universally condemned UK service levels, saying how bad we were at responding to requests for help and, as consumers, at complaining. So it is worth being aware that you need to be cognisant of your potential audience for any reports you issue – and their likely response. Another factor to consider is that, above all, customers in all spheres want honest, open, trustworthy data and communications in the course of their dealings with you.

What makes a good measure or metric?

Both the management quality gurus Edward Deming and Peter Drucker (and others, no one can agree who originally said it!) have been credited with saying 'what you can't measure you can't manage'. But there are as many conflicting views and opinions on what makes a good measurement of customer service as there are different ways of carrying out that measurement. Quantitative, qualitative, what customers think is important versus what we think is important internally, measuring the customer experience – which should be our focus for managing and delivering great service effectively?

> According to a [2008] global Nielsen survey of 26,486 internet users in 47 markets, consumer recommendations are the most credible form of advertising among 78 per cent of the study's respondents.
>
> - Trust in 'a person like me' far outranks any other institution, business, or spokesperson.
> - Consumers trust friends above experts when it comes to product recommendations (65% trust friends, 27% trust experts, 8% trust celebrities).
>
> (Resource Interactive and Bazaarvoice, 2008)

I believe strongly that the principles laid out in the introduction to this chapter – based on the customer (as per the 'trust issue' highlighted in the Nielsen survey above) and the business outcomes or improvement – must be your main focus. This applies whatever size your organization is – from a coffee kiosk in a station up to a multinational – although it is often easier to focus when you are smaller. In the past too many organizations have made the mistake of focusing on measuring things that do not relate – or matter – to either of these customer or business outcome principles. For example, in organizations with customer contact centres with telephony management systems, many measure statistics on calls per agent and time spent on a call. Although these are easy to track and can be good indicative measures of productivity, they are not sound measures of customer experience. It is often reported that some agents that have performance targets set in these areas can work harder to shorten calls and not work on building a rapport with customers – thereby directly reducing the quality of the customer interaction.

These types of measure do offer a day-to-day quantitative measure for supervisors of contact centre staff but are unable to provide any of the customer or business improvement feedback that customer service managers or company management will require. They certainly do not help to demonstrate the success or failure of the customer service team to help in the five areas identified in the introduction to this chapter. It does not demonstrate to the finance director that you are becoming more cost-effective, or show the marketing director that you are getting better customer feedback or driving customer behaviours, or the chief executive that you are a vital tool in growing the business and its profits.

In Chapter 6, we highlighted results of a study from Bright Index. In their 2009 *Performance Management Guide*, they identify three main areas where the highest-performing contact centres commonly measure performance (Figure 17).

EFFICIENCY	QUALITY	RESOURCING
• Cost per call • Calls per agent/ day • Self service • Sales	• Abandonment • Hold time • FCR [First Contact Resolution] • Agents per coach • Training	• Utilization • Attrition • Ready time (call time + wait) • Absence

Figure 17. Bright Performance Management Guide (2009).

You will notice that the measures of calls per agent and call time do appear here, but the report goes on to highlight that these high performing centres add two crucial further areas of measurement. These are employee satisfaction and engagement and customer satisfaction and behaviour. These are precisely the factors that we identified with the Harvard Service Profit Chain diagram in Chapter 3 and add customer and business meaning to the basic 'agent performance measures'.

These measures are now regarded as essential in larger organizations, but if you are a smaller operation, what can you do that will give you some meaningful data to help with customer retention and business improvement? In Chapter 5, I suggested the recording of customer complaints and suggestions as a basic record, but you might want to consider one of the independent 'rating' systems, such as those offered by eBay or TripAdvisor. At eBay they apply to the transaction experience and contribute to the trading record of both buyer and seller and are used extensively by businesses that are 'eBay traders'. At TripAdvisor, the destination and hotel guidance site, guests can rate eating or stay experiences. These types of 'customer support community' sites are likely to grow in popularity and could well provide smaller businesses with the customer feedback they desire. What is a particular benefit is that you capture the emotional feeling of the customer as well as any practical feedback on your services. That was one of the key areas identified in Chapter 2 as something customers wanted to be part of their great customer experience.

The Consultation Institute (TCI) offers the following opinion on such consumer feedback in its 'Tuesday topic' of 17 November 2009:

> Someone wishing to buy virtually any product or service these days can find the opinions of those who've already bought them. A good and thought-provoking example is 'Patient Opinion' – a site for users of the NHS to report on their experiences. The social enterprise responsible for this innovation has succeeded in persuading Health Managers to monitor what patients say and the benefits are obvious, but there is a concern that these sites attract the disaffected in disproportionate numbers. Yet 'Patient Opinion' (http://www.patientopinion.org.uk/) finds that 'thank you' postings are as frequent as critical comments.
>
> But is this really consultation? Few stories submitted by service users point to an obvious conclusion. When things go wrong, the fix is seldom straightforward. Ideally, therefore, gathering experiences should lead to a more productive analysis phase which might include some dialogue with those who have submitted their stories. They want to be heard, not just counted.
>
> All this forms part of the growing practice of customer consultation. Organizers of significant consultations with any stakeholder need to learn to distinguish between advice based upon experience and input based on other factors. They may also need to devise dialogue methods that suit different characteristics of evidence. In the emerging world of experience-informed engagement, the gatherers of customer stories have an honourable place, and public bodies of all kinds will need to work with them.

(The Consultation Institute, 2009)

What this current view from the consultation sector indicates is that there is a convergence of thinking across customer, consultee, citizen and consumer. There is little difference in the requirement to get feedback from whatever definition we care to apply to the 'customer'. So how does your organization gather customer stories? And what does it do with the information? Does it use it well enough? Does it use it at all? This is fundamental to the proliferation of customer data being gathered today – in the technology section we referred to CRM systems that offer many opportunities to gather and segment customer information. Some link into loyalty cards or other schemes that offer rewards to customers in return for 'belonging'. But is all the data used effectively to manage the service and make the offer to the customer better?

In the *Harvard Business Review* of September 2009, Dave Dougherty and Ajay Murthy reported on their recent research in 'What Service Customers Really Want'. Observing that 40 per cent of customers stop doing business with organizations that provide poor service, they recommend that 'managers should draw on a variety of information sources, including customer satisfaction surveys, behavioural data from self-service channels and recorded customer–agent conversations. In addition, they should revise processes to give agents leeway to meet individual customer needs and provide positive satisfying experiences' (Dougherty and Murthy, 2009). This very much underpins the Bright Index study and previous assertions in this book. I am convinced that keeping customer and business outcomes at the forefront of measures, gathering both performance and experiential data, and using analysis to identify business or product problem areas that require remedy or change is the recipe for determining true success or failure of customer service processes.

One area in which the customer is now able to provide more and more direct feedback to shape future services is in the public sector. Whether here in the UK or overseas, consultation with the relevant community of customers is now obligatory on all but the smallest changes to public services. Perhaps the most famous example is that of the White House in the USA. www.whitehouse.gov/blog/2009 is the home of public policy issues in all sorts of areas from health to transport and asks American citizens to contribute their ideas and views to shape future services. Here in the UK, www.number10.gov.uk performs the same function, and the Prime Minister invites YouTube questions which he will answer in the same way. This consultation culture is not just confined to central government: Barnet Council is experimenting with an 'EasyCouncil' concept to ask its citizens about service priorities in the likely future reduction of funds that councils will have to spend. They will be asked which services they would like to preserve, which they do not mind paying more towards or perhaps even dispensing with altogether. However, consultation is only effective if you listen to the answers – and are *seen* to be listening, either by feedback or by actions taken. Bad consultation is worse than none at all. You need to capture broad customer and market information to build into your customer service and business plan.

In capturing broader customer and citizen views, the UK leads the world in consultation best practice, and TCI has the most authoritative guidance in this area. For example, their 2008 best practice guide entitled *Effective Focus Groups* by Barry Creasy recommends how best to use these groups to gather data and information from people in this way. These groups are a direct mirror image of customer focus groups used in the private sector, and the information is therefore relevant to us all. Specific advice covers topics such as how many groups and who to invite, preparation and question types, how to moderate, record and report discussions and findings, and how to analyse and report conclusions.

In this section I have made the case for capturing and using customer feedback and information to guide your future activity in many areas – brand development, customer retention and loyalty, revenue protection and enhancement, business and product development and customer service team importance are the most prominent. I have also suggested that it is crucial to gather customer feedback and information from a wide selection of sources – not just CRM systems or contact centres, not just focus groups or consultation exercises, not just complaints, but a mix of what is most appropriate to your customers.

Anne Marie Forsyth, chief executive of the Customer Contact Association (see www.cca-global.com/), commented recently on looking beyond traditional measures.

> For many, measuring customer satisfaction is an essential part of an organisation's day to day management. Who can accept unhappy customers in a world of 'Watchdog' media coverage, Web 2.0 feedback and CEO demands that the 'customer comes first'? And how can service be improved if we don't measure what's broken?
>
> For the sceptics, loyalty or repeat spend are more important measures. Satisfied customers are known to defect, so some advocate the use of the Net Promoter Score. Others say CRM systems will (finally) capture the information needed to understand individual customer relationships with organisations; satisfaction will be one of many measures.
>
> (Bright Performance Management Guide, 2009)

Forsyth illustrates the need for a broad measurement of customer satisfaction, and has said that many of CCA's members are trying hard to get beyond the 'number of calls' type of measurement that means little to customers. There are no bad measures that are being used – but there are measures that are being used badly. I believe the simple 'customer view' test of value for a good customer measure or metric, as a précis of the guidance I have offered earlier in this section, is as follows:

- Will it help them (my product or service supplier) to stop doing things I do not like?
- Will it help them to do more of the things I like?
- Will it help them to make the product or service better, faster or cheaper?

That adds the customer viewpoint to test any measures or metrics you devise – and offers the incentive of self-interest to stay loyal to your brand and product or service. There is no guarantee that they will be retained, but it gives you the best possible chance to do so.

So, in conclusion, as we go on to look at how we might carry out measuring success or failure in our customer service operation, we now have both the determination of what is likely to make a good measure from the internal *and* external viewpoint. That is what makes a truly good measure.

What customer information do I need to collect, and how?

BS 8477 subclause 6.1.1 supports my assertion in the last section that a broad selection of sources should be used for customer feedback, including customers, employees, regular management checks/monitoring, audits, complaints and redress mechanisms, including ombudsmen. Subclause 6.1.2 goes on to specify customer focus groups, satisfaction surveys and other established methods. Subclause 6.1.3 adds obtaining employee suggestions and ideas through similar means and specifies that staff should receive feedback on action taken on their suggestions. This is all sound guidance and the standard also directly refers to mystery shopping to really get a customer perspective on how we are performing: 'Customer service employees should be regularly monitored/checked (e.g. through mystery shopping), to ensure that they are meeting an established level of customer service' (BS 8477: 2007).

In Chapter 5 we learned the value of complaints and compliments in terms of feedback, and BS ISO 10002 subclause 8.6 highlights not just how to review the complaints process but also how to use it for improving the use of complaints for 'proposals on product improvement and decisions and actions related to identified resource needs (e.g. training programmes)'. So standards have very much defined the path. How do you gather all of the varieties of customer feedback and information and then interpret what it means? Throughout the book I have referred to various methods of understanding customers, getting them to tell us what they like and don't like, giving us feedback on their 'experience' when in contact with our people, and our communication methods such as chat and websites. In this section, I am going to discuss my analysis on their effectiveness.

Personal experience: In smaller businesses, whether you have one or one hundred customers, the interaction you have with customers is your most valuable feedback mechanism. Even if you just keep a notebook with informal feedback – good and bad – it will provide a good base for analysis and learning where you could improve.

> **Case study 14: Jane Hext, Customer Services Director at Vodafone, on using automatic customer satisfaction surveys to drive change**
>
> Ensuring that performance management effectively motivates our people to put our customers first has been at the heart of transforming our culture in Vodafone. We have seen tremendous benefits from running daily real time customer satisfaction surveys sufficient for all advisers and teams to receive direct feedback from customers that they've spoken to which can be used to coach their skills development.
>
> The feedback and engagement from our advisers is overwhelmingly positive because they see us prioritising customer feedback far above traditional contact centre productivity metrics.
>
> The trick for all of us is trying to find a win–win performance management system. We have found that our people feel motivated and eager to know how our customers felt about their conversation, we gain valuable insight from the aggregated outcomes of the surveys and of course our customers appreciate that we care, as evidenced by the higher than normal response rate and volunteering of information.
>
> (Bright Performance Management Guide 2009)

Event-based survey: This survey allows you to track customer trends in satisfaction with current services and/or customer–employee interactions. They are regular, continual surveys (i.e. a follow-up email after a customer contact is closed). These surveys should be short (4–10 questions) and easy to complete quickly. This type of survey is one of the most effective ways to 'keep a finger on the pulse' of customer perception, and most CRM systems can do this automatically. Richer Sounds, the cut-price electrical chain, collects customer feedback in an innovative way – on the till receipt – and employees are incentivized to get the best feedback! One of the potential dangers with this type of survey is 'survey fatigue' where, for example, customers tire of filling in comment forms in hotel rooms. You may only then receive feedback from customers you have really impressed – or really upset – which means your results will not be representative.

One-time/one-off survey: This survey is not completed at regularly scheduled intervals but undertaken for specific reasons such as a change in product or service provided. It is a very valuable tool to use after a series of complaints, implementation of new services or major changes to products or groups of customers.

Social media and community-based networks: As highlighted in Chapter 6, these networks offer the opportunity to discover B2C and B2B community feedback on brands and company image and to gain valid and fresh customer feedback on your products and services. Taking control of this media, rather than reacting to it, is important and many organizations already allocate resources for this. Online reviews and forums are now one of the first ports of call for customers seeking advice from others who are willing to share their experience. Monitoring these networks is beneficial, but I believe there is no current case to invest in these technologies further than that. Dell, which suffered a dramatic loss of confidence in its products and services in 2005, due to online blogs undermining confidence in the brand, used and monitored blogging to help improve their customer feedback and loyalty.

Periodic/annual survey: This survey is planned and scheduled on a periodic basis, normally part of the annual budget cycle. Sometimes they are undertaken twice a year or quarterly. They are generally based on customer perception of the organization and the customer service during the last year or the period since the last survey of this type was undertaken. This type of survey should measure the same elements and allow an organization to see trends in service improvements year on year. An excellent example from the Nominet Registrant Customer Satisfaction Survey, 2007, is shown in Figures 18 and 19. This survey has identified both what is important to customers and how Nominet, who manage all internet domain names in the UK, performed against those important areas.

To learn more about the science and detail of surveying customers, I recommend *Customer Surveying* by Frederick C. Van Bennekom (2002), which examines and advises on every aspect of surveying customers, including key advice on the validity of the survey 'instrument'. He states that there are crucial questions to answer for each survey you take, such as 'Do the questions on the instrument truly measure what we intend them to measure?' and 'Does every respondent interpret the questions on the instrument in the same way?'

Measurement of customer service success 131

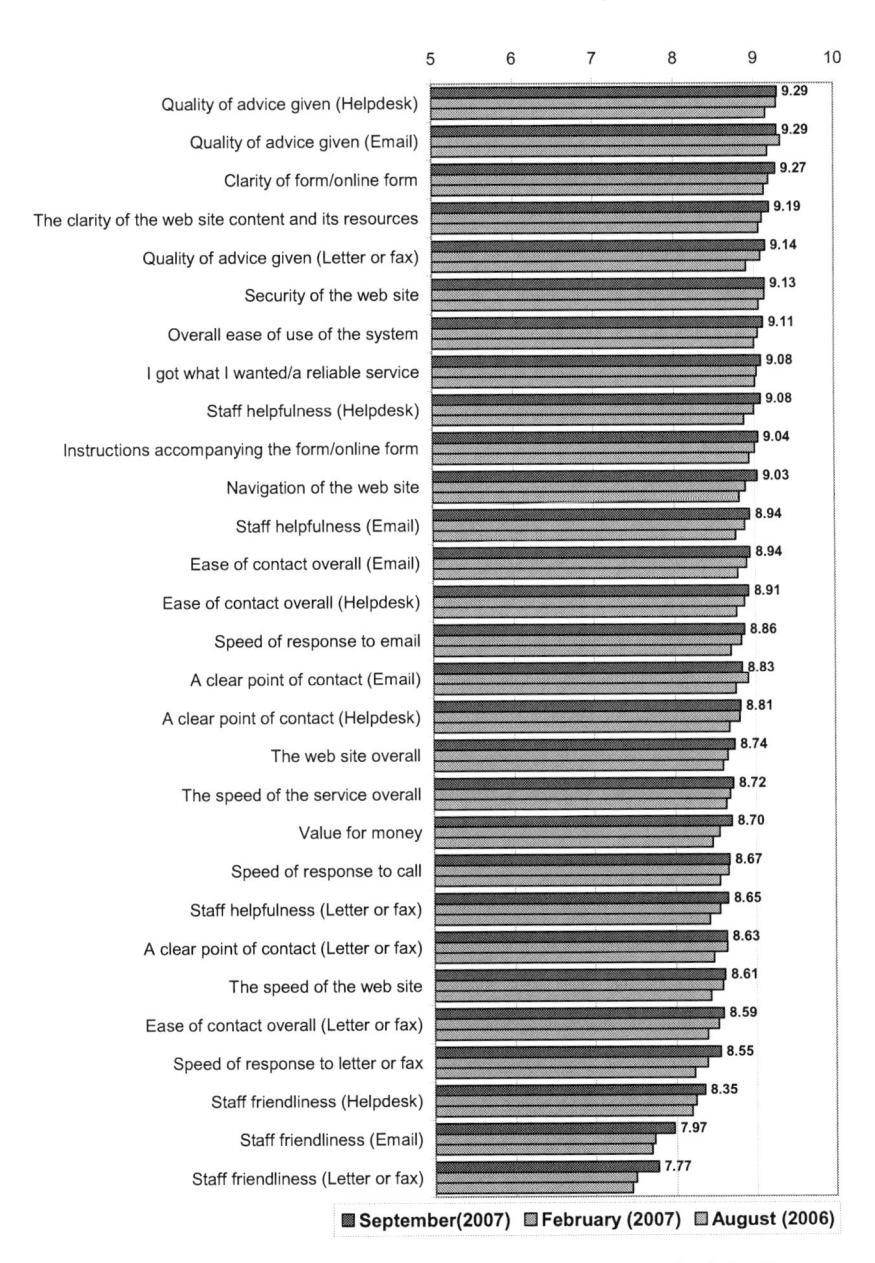

Category	Rating
Quality of advice given (Helpdesk)	9.29
Quality of advice given (Email)	9.29
Clarity of form/online form	9.27
The clarity of the web site content and its resources	9.19
Quality of advice given (Letter or fax)	9.14
Security of the web site	9.13
Overall ease of use of the system	9.11
I got what I wanted/a reliable service	9.08
Staff helpfulness (Helpdesk)	9.08
Instructions accompanying the form/online form	9.04
Navigation of the web site	9.03
Staff helpfulness (Email)	8.94
Ease of contact overall (Email)	8.94
Ease of contact overall (Helpdesk)	8.91
Speed of response to email	8.86
A clear point of contact (Email)	8.83
A clear point of contact (Helpdesk)	8.81
The web site overall	8.74
The speed of the service overall	8.72
Value for money	8.70
Speed of response to call	8.67
Staff helpfulness (Letter or fax)	8.65
A clear point of contact (Letter or fax)	8.63
The speed of the web site	8.61
Ease of contact overall (Letter or fax)	8.59
Speed of response to letter or fax	8.55
Staff friendliness (Helpdesk)	8.35
Staff friendliness (Email)	7.97
Staff friendliness (Letter or fax)	7.77

■ September(2007) ■ February (2007) ■ August (2006)

Figure 18. Customer importance rating (Nominet Registrant Satisfaction Survey, 2007).

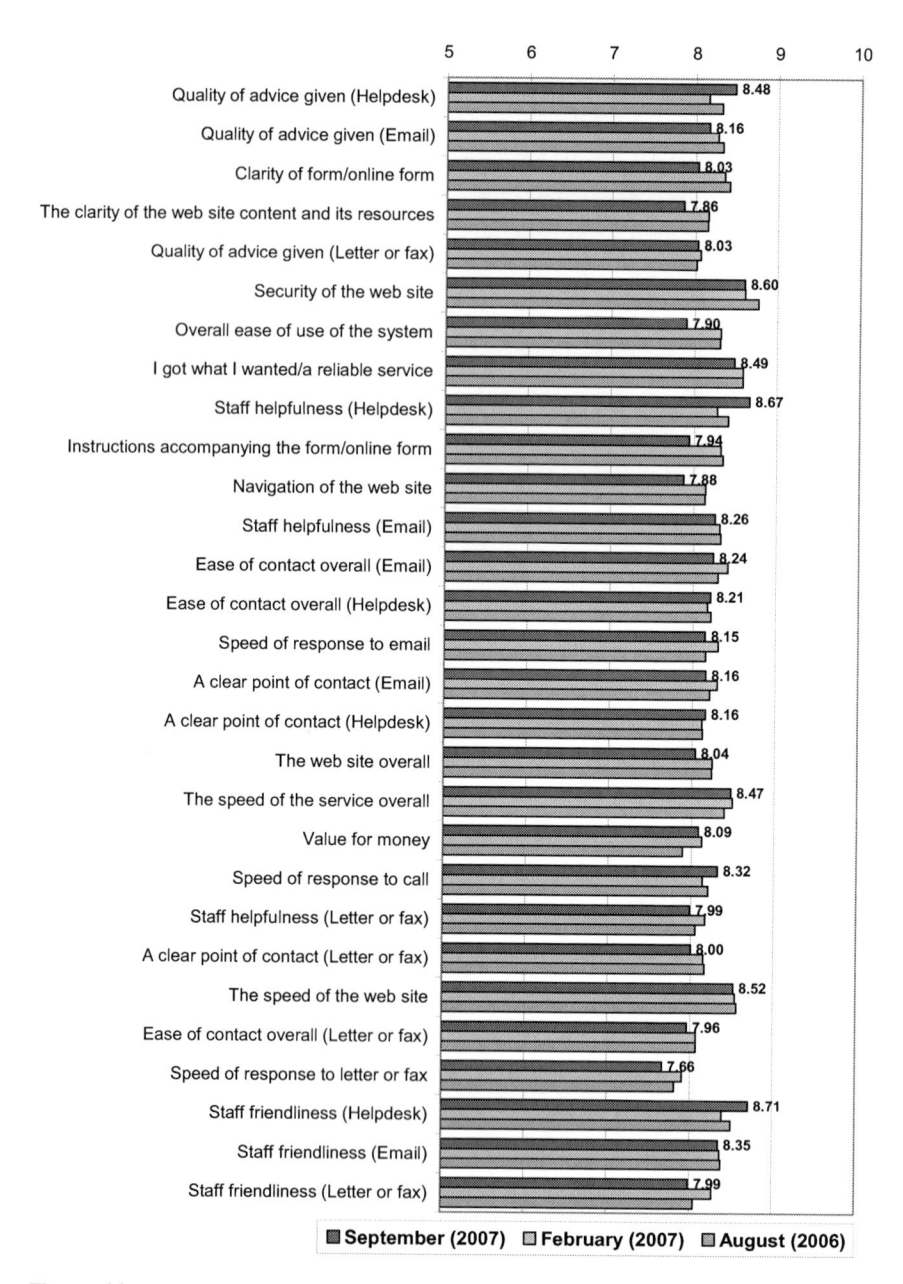

132 *Quality Service, Competitive Business: setting the standard in customer service*

Category	Value
Quality of advice given (Helpdesk)	8.48
Quality of advice given (Email)	8.16
Clarity of form/online form	8.03
The clarity of the web site content and its resources	7.86
Quality of advice given (Letter or fax)	8.03
Security of the web site	8.60
Overall ease of use of the system	7.90
I got what I wanted/a reliable service	8.49
Staff helpfulness (Helpdesk)	8.67
Instructions accompanying the form/online form	7.94
Navigation of the web site	7.88
Staff helpfulness (Email)	8.26
Ease of contact overall (Email)	8.24
Ease of contact overall (Helpdesk)	8.21
Speed of response to email	8.15
A clear point of contact (Email)	8.16
A clear point of contact (Helpdesk)	8.16
The web site overall	8.04
The speed of the service overall	8.47
Value for money	8.09
Speed of response to call	8.32
Staff helpfulness (Letter or fax)	7.99
A clear point of contact (Letter or fax)	8.00
The speed of the web site	8.52
Ease of contact overall (Letter or fax)	7.96
Speed of response to letter or fax	7.66
Staff friendliness (Helpdesk)	8.71
Staff friendliness (Email)	8.35
Staff friendliness (Letter or fax)	7.99

■ September (2007) □ February (2007) ▨ August (2006)

Figure 19. Registrant customer satisfaction (Nominet Registrant Customer Satisfaction Survey, 2007).

It is often essential to incentivize customer feedback by offering a bottle of champagne, free products or a fashionable electronic device. This should ensure that a reasonable percentage of the sample will respond and help to circumvent 'survey fatigue'. The other possibility is to be innovative about the way you get feedback – as mentioned earlier, at Richer Sounds they include a short service feedback section on the till receipt, and staff are incentivized on service levels and so are keen to ask customers to fill it in. Incentives – or at least a nice venue that customers would like to visit – will also help with the group sessions below.

Focus groups: A focus group is a select group of customers that meets and discusses predetermined issues. There will be someone from the service team, or possibly an independent facilitator or chairperson, leading the questioning of the group, taking minutes and reporting the findings back to the team. It is a great way to explore the key customer issues you need to address when you plan the way forward for customer service.

Round table discussions: These bring customers together to raise issues or concerns in an open forum and the only agenda is to get the customers' views. These sessions differ from focus groups because the customers determine what issues will be covered. They are a good way of capturing customer information in an informal and unscripted way.

Website monitoring, polls and customer 'rating' requests: There are many tools available today (see Chapter 6) to monitor and measure what customers are doing on your website, how long they stay, what pages they visit and more. Google Analytics is one such option. You can also set criteria to ask customers questions about their experience on the site and get them to 'rate' the visit or order. This is all really useful information, but if you are planning to collect it, you must consider whether, especially if it requires customer input, it is intrusive or if it is adding value to your collected information. Setting clear goals – as with the other forms of collection here – is crucial. If, for example, you can use the data to determine what customers particularly like about one part or feature of your site, that can be used to bring other areas to that standard. Using 'rating' requests, such as those mentioned earlier from eBay or TripAdvisor, after a purchase or customer interaction, are great for assessing how well your organization performed. They do, however, need to be specific on what customers liked or did not like to be truly useful.

To emphasize the importance of user generated content (UGC), a 2008 Bazaarvoice and Resource Interactive research report found that 53 per cent of online retailers currently utilize UGC on their site. Of these UGC adopters, 78 per cent have implemented ratings and reviews, 39 per cent have implemented testimonials, and 39 per cent have implemented discussion boards or forums. Almost three-quarters of retailers said that UGC is important to their overall business. Respondents mostly expect their investment to impact conversion rate, customer satisfaction and customer loyalty. Figure 20 illustrates that over 70 per cent of responders think that this type of data is fairly important to their businesses.

Importance of UGC to Business

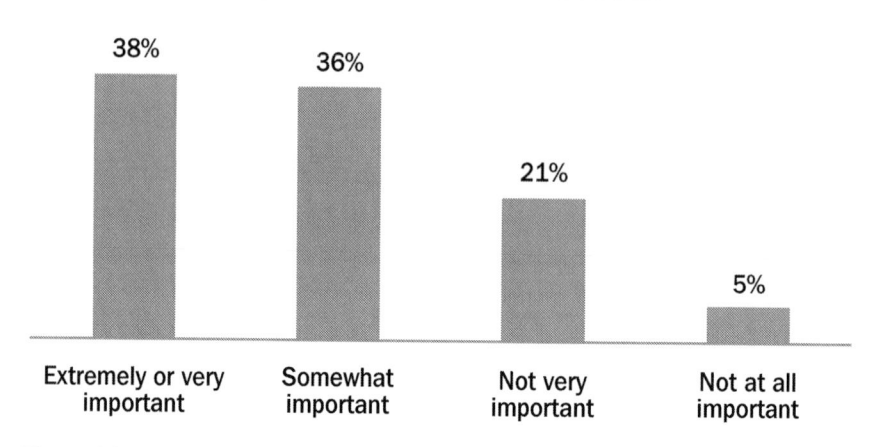

- Extremely or very important: 38%
- Somewhat important: 36%
- Not very important: 21%
- Not at all important: 5%

Figure 20. Importance of UGC to business, (Resource Interactive, and Bazaar Voice, 2008).

The same retailers identified the impact of UGC (Figure 21) and showed that increased conversion rates, increased customer satisfaction and increased customer loyalty are the actual and anticipated business metrics most impacted by online UGC. The percentages indicate the two highest impact measures from a five-point impact scale.

Customer telephone contact monitoring: As identified in Chapter 6, the recording (you are legally obliged to tell customers this is happening) and use of customer calls for learning about customer behaviour and staff performance is invaluable. It provides input for staff development programmes as well as helping to understand customers. It takes significant time and expense to do well and hence should only be an option for 20-seat or larger contact centres.

Net promoter score: This customer loyalty metric was developed by Fred Reicheld, Bain and company and Satmetrix and is used by several organizations, including Microsoft and Amazon. It suggests that customer loyalty and retention is vital and is based on the fundamental question: 'How likely are you to recommend us to a friend or colleague?' The responses are then charted on a rating scale of 0–10, with 0 being the least likely to recommend and 10 being the most likely to recommend. Customers are then divided into promoters (score 9–10), passives (7–8) and detractors (0–6). The score is obtained by ignoring the passives – as they are regarded as unlikely to promote or detract – and subtracting detractors from promoters. Although the score should be permanently in positive territory, it is not the simple 'once and for all' measure that supporters suggest. However, it is a good measure to include in your broad selection.

Impact of UGC

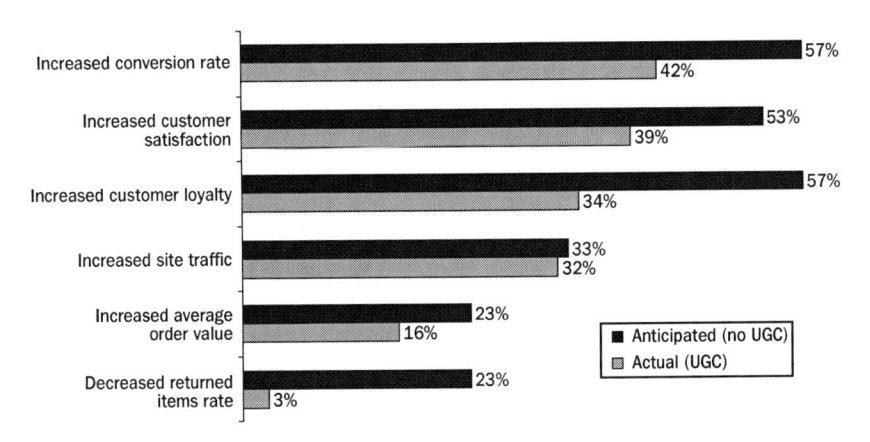

Metric	Anticipated (no UGC)	Actual (UGC)
Increased conversion rate	42%	57%
Increased customer satisfaction	39%	53%
Increased customer loyalty	34%	57%
Increased site traffic	32%	33%
Increased average order value	16%	23%
Decreased returned items rate	3%	23%

Figure 21. Impact of UGC (Resource Interactive, and Bazaar Voice, 2008).

Shaun Smith (2009) of Smith & Co wrote in his white paper *Ten Lessons to Succeed with CEM Now, Rather Than Wait for the Next Big Thing* that:

> measuring the customer experience was essential. CEO Andy Taylor and his team at US-based Enterprise Rent-A-Car only focus on one thing; the number of customers who give the highest rating for satisfaction and are willing to recommend the company to others. Enterprise enjoys both the highest rate of growth and, at near 35 per cent, the highest net-promoter percentage in the car-rental industry according to Reichheld. World-class organizations like Amazon.com have net-promoter scores of 75-80 per cent. However, what is really important is to reward the KPIs that you want to move. And that takes us to our last point – that aligning your KPIs with the customer experience is essential.
>
> (www.smithcoconsultancy.com/, 2009)

Mystery shopping: This has already been mentioned in earlier chapters as a good way to see how your customers are likely to be faring when they are in contact with your business. It can be used to evaluate every customer contact process from website navigation and ordering to face-to-face store service. It can be done through 'friends and family' in a smaller business, or through a specialist agency for larger organizations. The senior management team can participate in their own customer experience sampling through the 'back to the floor' approach, serving and interacting with customers and first-line staff.

Benchmarks: These are primarily used by organizations to compare how well they are doing against either 'the industry' or their peers in their business sector. They can be offered by industry associations such as the Institute of Customer Service, SDI or the CCA, or independently by organizations such as the Bright Index or Dimension Data. Although not directly telling whether you are good or bad, it will allow you to establish whether you are performing better or worse than others and whether you have improved since the last study. It is important to ensure that the right key performance indicators (KPIs) are included for your service operation and customers and that the data sources are both reliable and relevant. First contact resolution figures from SDI (Figure 22) show how report data can vary.

Metric	Figures	Sources
First Contact Resolution	(Average) 59%	HDI Best Practices Benchmarking Report (2007)
	Variation of 72% – 98%	Bright on behalf of Service Futures Group (2006)
	(Average) 85%	Bright on behalf of Service Futures Group (2006)
	(Average) 83%	The Merchants Global Contact Centre Benchmarking Report 2006
	(Average) 71%	Dimension Data The Merchants Global Contact Centre Benchmarking Report 2006

Figure 22. SDI service desk metrics report (2007).

You will also want to consider the peer group against whom you would like to be 'benchmarked' – the same type of business, businesses of the same size, comparable sectors, etc. All of the providers will be able to guide you on this.

In conclusion, there is so much potential data to collect, and there are so many ways to collect it, that the challenge really is to decide what you want to achieve from the measures and then to select those that fit your goals best. In general, I believe the core reasons for customer service measurement and reporting are to keep customers happy in the short term and improve customer loyalty and service and product quality over the long term. I would recommend a short automatic electronic customer survey and personal experience for the short term, and an annual satisfaction survey and net promoter score for the longer term. For a larger business, I would add web and speech monitoring to understand how customers are interacting with my business and how my staff members are performing. I would also add periodic focus groups and benchmarking exercises to establish trends and gain direct customer input. I would continually go 'back to the floor', and ask friends to mystery shop my own business if small or use an agency if larger. However, that is a personal view and you need to develop your own mix. If you are in doubt, your industry association will be able to advise you.

Analysis, interpretation and reporting

Once you have collected your data, you need to be able to make sense of what you have collected and to draw conclusions from it. Although that seems obvious, many customer service operations stop at the level of simply reporting sets of numbers – often in a quite 'disconnected' fashion. This will establish quantitative trends, but it will be unlikely to determine whether customers intend to stay with you or whether your service offerings are improving. There are many ways to present information, from a simple spreadsheet to a more formal report that includes graphs, charts, dashboards and quadrant diagrams. They all offer variations of how to present your data so that it can be analysed and interpreted to best effect. The options you choose will be influenced by your goals and requirements determined earlier in this chapter and by advice from experts and industry associations.

Looking back to the variety of measures and how they might be interpreted, a report by Unica relating to the use of web analytics shows how you could look at customer web data across their life cycle with your business (Figure 23).

Figure 23 shows the central 'marketer's goals' throughout the customer lifecycle and on the right the possible actions that could be carried out. This model could be adapted for any customer service operation in order to get the best from its customer data. The example from Nominet discussed earlier in the chapter shows how it has established the importance to the customer of particular aspects of their service before reporting levels of satisfaction. This ensures that the customer view is always pre-eminent and should form part of your thinking when analysing data. Fujitsu, the IT services business, places a lot of store by its customer feedback, and in the customer satisfaction report (Figure 24; Case study 15) has drawn together several customer responses into a simple summary form.

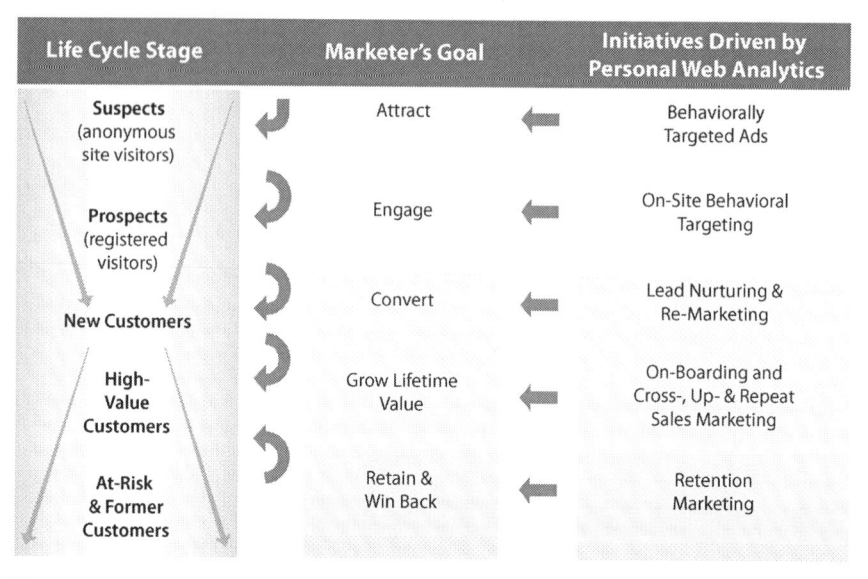

Life Cycle Stage	Marketer's Goal	Initiatives Driven by Personal Web Analytics
Suspects (anonymous site visitors)	Attract	Behaviorally Targeted Ads
Prospects (registered visitors)	Engage	On-Site Behavioral Targeting
New Customers	Convert	Lead Nurturing & Re-Marketing
High-Value Customers	Grow Lifetime Value	On-Boarding and Cross-, Up- & Repeat Sales Marketing
At-Risk & Former Customers	Retain & Win Back	Retention Marketing

Figure 23. Mapping life cycle stages and business goals to initiatives that can be driven by personal web analytics (Unica, 2009).

Customer:		Scorecard Period:	Q4-Jan			
Department:	Business Services	Year:	2009			
Contact:	Business Representative	Date Completed:	27/01/2009			
CATEGORY	SUB-CATEGORY	CUSTOMER COMMENTS	Actual Score	Importance	Weighted Score	Category Weighted Score
Vision & Strategy	How satisfied are you that Fujitsu Services supports your aims and objectives?					8.0
Contract & Value	How satisfied are you that the contract(s) delivers to your expectations?					8.0
Relationships	How satisfied are you with the relationships you have with Fujitsu?					8.2
Resources	How satisfied are you with our people?					8.6
Service	How satisfied are you that the service(s) supplied provides business benefit?					8.0
Projects and Change	How satisfied are you that project and change management meets your requirements?					7.8
OVERALL	Overall, how satisfied are you with Fujitsu Services,			8.09		25
	On a scale of 1–10 where 4 is dissatisfied and 7 is satisfied					7

Figure 24. SDI Fujitsu 2009 Excellence Awards entry.

Customer:		Scorecard Period:	Q4-Jan		
Department:	Business Services	Year:	2009		
Contact:	Business Representative	Date Completed:	27/01/2009		

CATEGORY	SUB-CATEGORY	CUSTOMER COMMENTS	Actual Score	Impor- tance	Weighted Score	Category Weighted Score
Business Development	What can Fujitsu Services do to improve its standing in your organisation?					
	Get the core service delivery right and deliver to expectations on transformation & then demonstrate added value. Be a seamless part of Group IT					
	How can Fujitsu best develop & grow to the benefit of both organisations?					
	Develop a deep understanding of what's important to the Bank, particularly the BUs, and deliver the required service perfectly/excellently. Then offer new services to help our organisation succeed					
Reference	How likely are you to recommend Fujitsu to another customer					7
	On a scale of 1–10 where 4 is unlikely and 7 is likely					

Figure 24. SDI Fujitsu 2009 Excellence Awards entry *(continued)*.

> **Case study 15: Fujitsu customer satisfaction measures**
>
> For key stakeholders we use an independent and objective 3rd party. This 3rd party conducts a CSIP (Customer Satisfaction Interview Programme) with customers who are named key contacts. Face-to-face interviews are conducted on an annual basis (although some customers prefer for this to be more frequent) and aim to provide an environment for the customer to be honest about the services provided.
>
> For the specific Business Units the Service Delivery Managers complete reviews with the relevant customer Service Manager in order to complete a set Customer Satisfaction Scorecard. The Service Desk distributes question forms to a selection of client staff who have logged calls in order to measure the satisfaction levels of the users of the Service Desk. The results of the responses are then compiled to provide overall satisfaction scores for the Service Desk as above.
>
> (SDI Fujitsu 2009 Excellence Awards Entry)

Case study 15 shows how relevant data relating to customers can be pulled together for analysis. Whether to do this on an annual or more regular basis will be decided between yourselves and your customers.

'Dashboards' are another popular way of showing a group of measures that might illustrate good or bad performance in your chosen data.

The Bright Performance Management Guide (2009) shows data presented in a 'speedometer' style with a red 'poor' zone on the left, amber in the middle and green in the 'good' zone on the right of each scale. The 'traffic light' system is an excellent way of drawing attention to those areas requiring attention. It makes interpretation simple and can be qualified by accompanying text.

Using and promoting outcomes effectively

Whether internal or external, the use of the data collected and presented is vital both in 'closing the loop' with customers and in the promotion of the customer service ethos and team internally in your organization. Strativity's 2009 *Global Customer Experience Management Benchmark Study* report recognizes the difficulty of achieving action when using customer feedback data (Figure 25).

This difficulty may indicate the lack of real commitment to the customer, or more likely a general resistance to change. Both are undesirable, and customer measurement and reporting can provide an 'alert' relating to these concerns, which should be a catalyst for remedial action. Customers rightly expect data that they have spent time and effort giving you on how they rate you as a supplier to be used effectively and to generate action or change. Failure to act breaks down the trust they have in you and the 'implied promise' that you will use their feedback. The Strativity Report mentioned on the previous page supports my assertion that complete commitment at all levels of the organization is essential to deliver good customer service. For it to be 'great' it will require that commitment to be ongoing.

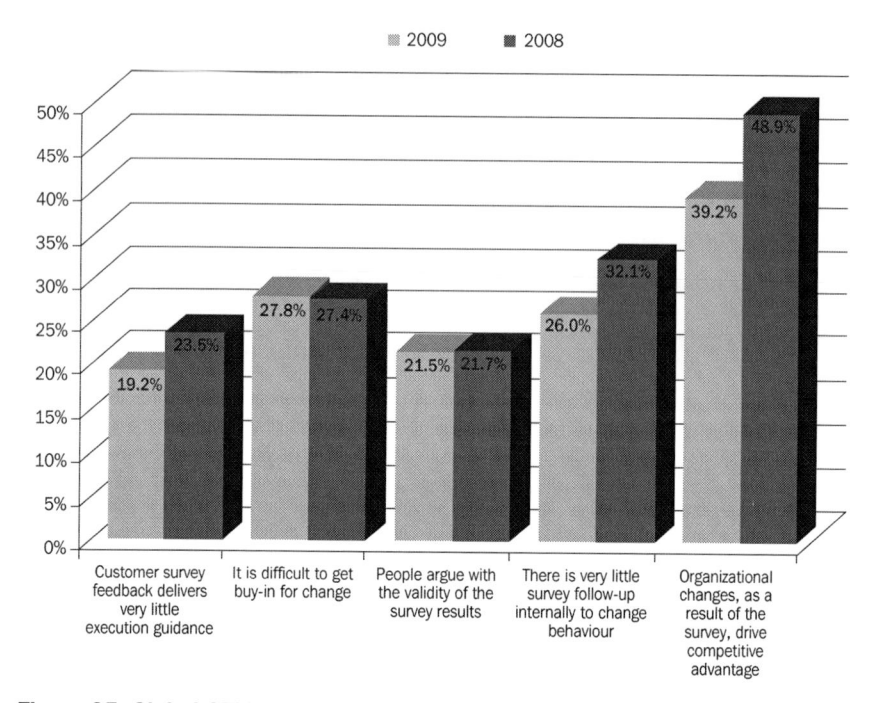

	2009	2008
Customer survey feedback delivers very little execution guidance	19.2%	23.5%
It is difficult to get buy-in for change	27.8%	27.4%
People argue with the validity of the survey results	21.5%	21.7%
There is very little survey follow-up internally to change behaviour	26.0%	32.1%
Organizational changes, as a result of the survey, drive competitive advantage	39.2%	48.9%

Figure 25. Global CEM Benchmark Study, May 2009, Strativity Group.

The Strativity Report states that management 'need to design their voice of customer programmes with "actionability" in mind' (2009). It goes on to list the typical action steps required:

> Companies need to demonstrate to their employees how listening and responding to customer insight and feedback creates a competitive advantage; Customer surveys should be designed to affect change internally and create competitive advantage; Survey results should be linked to actual customer behaviour (spend, share of wallet, attrition, etc.) to enable the company to compare the behaviour of loyal or satisfied customers to that of other customers, helping build a business case for increasing customer loyalty; 'Voice of customer' programmes should serve as a method of

building trust with customers by acting on their insight and communicating change back to them; Customer loyalty scores should be tied to employee compensation to align employee incentives with customer satisfaction.

(Global CEM Benchmark Study, 2009)

John Lewis (including its Waitrose supermarket brand) has long been regarded as a leading retailer with great customer service, and has worked tirelessly to keep that reputation. It uses an automated customer satisfaction system to collect and report on real-time customer satisfaction related issues. Case study 16 illustrates the outcomes.

Case study 16: John Lewis – Britain's Favourite Retailer 2009

'John Lewis has been voted Britain's favourite retailer in a poll of over 6,000 shoppers. The survey, carried out by retail analysts Verdict Research, ranks John Lewis first for customer satisfaction … Customers were asked to rank high street shops on a number of key criteria: range, price, convenience, quality, service, ambience, facilities and layout.'

(http://www.johnlewis.com/Help/Help.aspx?HelpId=4#UK's%20favourite, 2009)

John Lewis's system uses elements of supplier eDigitalResearch's eMysteryShopper, specializing in the study of website usability, functionality, and customer service. Another product, eCustomerOpinions, also provides feedback, but directly from randomly selected web site visitors. Customers' views have driven the development of Waitrose's By Invitation and WaitroseDeliver services, and Quick Check, the scan-as-you shop service. In John Lewis, name badges were introduced for selling Partners to make customer service more personal, in response to customers saying they wanted to remember who had helped them, in case they wanted to return for further help.

(http://www.edigitalresearch.com/news/item/nid/993081879, 2006, and http://www.johnlewispartnership.co.uk/Display.aspx?MasterId=1c4e8a06-26bb-4452-a574-378d4e0d82e4&NavigationId=629)

'[The system] collects customer purchase information from the John Lewis database and emails surveys out to customers, tying in all the purchase information with customer responses. Monthly reports are produced which can be cross-tabbed and filtered in terms of product groups (identifying which products are exceeding expectations and which may be falling short). Reports specific to particular divisions of John Lewis are also produced. John Ashton, Head of Direct Marketing at John Lewis says: "Divisions can examine issues relating directly to them, for example, the Operations Division can compare direct customer feedback on standards of delivery with the sugared feedback sometimes produced by third-party couriers."'

(http://www.marketresearchtech.com/edigitalresearch-guest-satisfaction-john-lewis.htm, Undated)

The John Lewis example is typical of the attention to detail shown by organizations with reputations for great service, which becomes more difficult to deliver when the business grows and control over the remote stores and staff is challenging. The provision of specific divisional feedback to allow them to keep a service focus and improvement policy alive is excellent.

Having started this chapter with a reference to CEO level 'results that matter', I will close it with how CEOs and boards should collate and use their customer feedback. The website www.mycustomer.com carried a recent report on measuring and using customer satisfaction and Figure 26 illustrates how feedback can be used across the organization to improve loyalty and help drive down costs.

Figure 26 uses RFA systems to make its point. These systems are often integrated with e-business applications, to gather feedback periodically or as soon as customers have been served. Analytics, verbatim suggestions and other intelligence are delivered to the right employees who can act on them in real time. Business rules ensure that no customer is surveyed excessively and that enough feedback is gathered for results to be meaningful. The point to remember is that, as in the John Lewis example, it is the action taken as a result that is crucial. As highlighted in Chapter 6, it is all too easy to allow technology to 'be our solution' and not overlay the human and common sense interpretation needed to make the best use of customer feedback data.

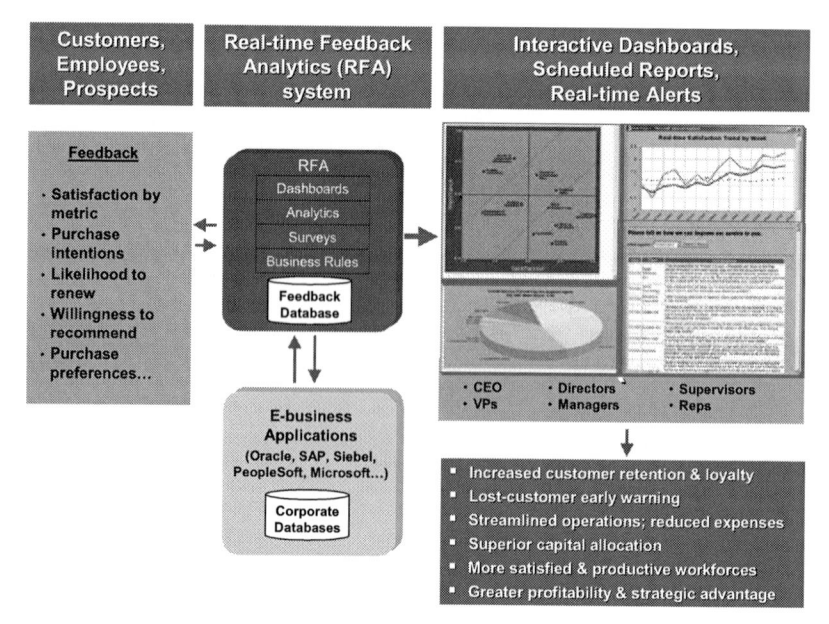

Figure 26. Real-time feedback analytics (RFA) systems and benefits, (CustomerSat, 2009) at: http://www.mycustomer.com/files/siftmedia-mycustomer/customersat-002.pdf.

Summary

This chapter has been designed not just to identify how you might measure and demonstrate success in customer service, but also to close the loop on the entire customer service model and process. It is no exaggeration to say that customer service holds the key to the future of your organization, as loyal and returning customers buying an improved product and good service *are* that future. No organization can afford to have many United Airlines–YouTube moments, as the resulting loss of revenues, customers and reputation are impossible to bear if it is more than an isolated occurrence. Customers want simple, honest, effective service and to be listened to when they have an opinion. This chapter has shown you how to use those opinions and also how to monitor and report on the interactions that give rise to those opinions.

BS 8477 emphasizes how important it is to have a process to monitor and evaluate how well your service is performing. In this chapter we emphasize the crucial aspects within that, especially those of supporting your brand image, supporting long-term customer loyalty and business improvement and raising the profile and importance of the customer service team and mission.

Learning points

- Capture and use of customer feedback on the quality of service is the only way to 'close the loop' and to ensure the future of the business through improved products and services and customer loyalty.
- Measures and metrics that do not directly address either improved customer satisfaction or business improvement elements (number of calls handled per employee, for example) should add value to a broader mix of relevant measures or be discontinued.
- Clear goals for the outcome of your customer service success measures are essential for your analysis and interpretation.
- Getting genuine customer views in addition to any automated metrics keeps data honest and relevant – the use of consultation and personal experience data is crucial to elicit those views, which should be listened to and acted upon to retain customer trust.
- Using a combination of customer feedback data collection methods and tools, including senior management going 'back to the floor', will avoid customer 'survey fatigue' and provide strategic customer data to work with.

- Establishing what the customer thinks is important, as in the Nominet example, is an excellent way to keep customer wishes at the forefront of your success measures and thinking.
- Promoting the outcomes of measuring customer success data is critical for keeping focus and commitment of the internal organization to service – and also to demonstrate actions on customer feedback to them.

The following is a short list of techniques and examples to consider and learn from.

Techniques

- The use of customer consultation techniques, such as focus groups and meetings, should add to the mix of survey and automated feedback gathered from customers.
- In the same way, monitoring social media sites will add unexpurgated social 'chatter' and feedback on brand and product perception in the marketplace.
- Mystery shopping ensures that the customer's point of view, when contacting and dealing with your organization, is always at the forefront of your thinking.
- The use of a net promoter score as part of a broad and balanced mix of customer success measures gives customer loyalty a clear emphasis.
- The presentation of customer feedback data and other related performance or staff productivity data in a 'dashboard' style or 'traffic light' summary allows the highlighting of issues of concern.
- At Marval, a software business in the IT service market, they ask each of their team leaders to report on service deliverables each week, highlighting their team's two areas for improvement; one main area of success; one thing another team could do to help them do their job better; one thing their team could do to help other teams; one thing they could do to deliver an improved service to customers; and one thing they would change if they were the boss. This technique is similar to that used by John Lewis in Case study 16.
- Benchmarking – or at the very least spending time observing the way others in your or comparative industries provide service – is invaluable in determining where you are on the 'success' scale.

Examples

- Advertising for Microsoft Windows 7 emphasizes how it delivers new functionality that the customer asked for, using customer feedback to help design the product.

- In *Direct from Dell*, Michael Dell highlights how they ensure that 300,000 customers have 'their pulse taken each week' to get feedback.
- Customer analytics – speech or website – are becoming increasingly used to evaluate customer interaction as with eBay and TripAdvisor business or trader style ratings. Organizations such as Enterprise Rent-a-Car , Vodafone and John Lewis are all using these effectively to improve their service.
- The UKCSI survey example quoting ever improving UK service shows the danger of asking a narrow and self-interested sample to comment, and then offering the results to others who have not participated.
- The Richer Sounds till receipt method of customer feedback is simple and easily replicable.

Conclusion

At the start of this book, I set out to write a straightforward, easy-to-read book that confirms all that you *should* know about customer service and challenges you to think about what you need to learn and actions you need to take to make it better for you and your customers. I have researched extensively, drawn on the best of BSI, ISO and other industry standards and expert advice, used current and past examples and case studies to illustrate key learning points and identified further reading in the bibliography.

I believe that I have met my goal and I hope you feel the same. I think it is important to summarize and reinforce some of the key things you need to remember.

1. Follow the chapters – the book has been written in the order in which I believe you should address the issue of customer service in your organization. This applies whether you run a coffee stall in your local market or a large multinational business.
2. Understand customers – more specifically, *your* customers. Your organization exists only to serve them, and you need to understand their key priorities for service, both now and in the future. However you deliver to or interact with customers, there are things that they like or dislike, want you to do more of, or less of. Unless you know which apply to your customers, you are making it more difficult for your organization to serve and keep them.
3. What is great service? Despite having sought customer views, established what you think it is, and experienced service from others, no one other than you, or your organization, can decide the service levels and customer experience that you will give your customers. And, equally important, can you afford to deliver premium levels of service compared with your competitors? Or possibly can you afford *not* to do so?
4. Your service plan – influenced heavily by the points above, will define the level of service your organization wants, and can afford, to deliver. You

should consider how you will profitably, or within budget, seek to meet the expectations of customers. This will require careful planning, diligent and enthusiastic execution, ongoing monitoring and continual improvement as expectations are rising all the time.

5. The right people – from our own experiences we have encountered both good and bad customer service people. You need yours to be good! However, that is incredibly difficult to achieve consistently. Selection based on service attitudes and behaviours will help, but leadership, implementing and maintaining a service-orientated culture, and giving staff a motivated and 'fun' environment will be essential.

6. Processes and technology – the former is essential to form the bedrock of stability when business, customers, staff and technology will be changing and to define responsibilities and ways of doing customer service well. The latter will be both a help and a hindrance to the processes. In helping you to capture, track and analyse customer data it will be invaluable. In making customer feedback and communication much faster and more visible, business is impacted and needs to react much more quickly. 2009, for example, saw the reputations of banks, governments and well-known sports or show business celebrities such as Tiger Woods and Jonathan Ross, tarnished by the power of communication and social and customer media.

7. Measure your success and never stand still – at any given time you need to know what level of performance success and customer satisfaction you are achieving against the goals that you have set yourself. From that assessment you need to improve continually, preferably faster than both your customers expect and definitely more than your competitors.

If you are able, and want, to ingrain the learning points from the book in yourself and your organization's culture and approach – and exhibit the attitudes and behaviours recommended – it will help you to achieve both a successful career and a thriving customer-led organization.

Bibliography

Books

Barlow, J and Moller, C (1996) *A Complaint is a Gift*, San Francisco: Berrett-Koehler
Barlow, N (2006) *Re-think: How to Think Differently*, Chichester: Capstone
Blanchard, K and Bowles S (1996) *Raving Fans*, San Francisco: Jossey-Bass
Buckingham, M. and Clifton, D (2001) *Now, Discover Your Strengths*, New York: Free Press
Buckingham, M and Clifton, D (2008) 'The traces of talent', in J Gallos (ed.) *Business Leadership: A Jossey-Bass Reader*, San Francisco: Jossey-Bass
Carlzon, J (1987) *Moments of Truth*, Stockholm: Harper Perennial
Daffy, C (2001) *Once a Customer, Always a Customer*, Dublin: Oak Tree
Dell, M (1999) *Direct from Dell: Strategies that Revolutionized an Industry*, New York: Harper Collins
Freemantle, D (2004) *The Buzz: 50 Little Things That Make a Big Difference to Serve Your Customer*, London: Nicholas Brealey Publishing
Heskett, JL, Sasser, WE and Schlesinger, LA (1997) *The Service Profit Chain: How Leading Companies Link Profit and Growth to Loyalty, Satisfaction, and Value*, New York: Free Press
Gober, M (1999) *The Art of Giving Quality Service*, Clarence, NY: Gober & Associates International
Goleman, D (1995) *Emotional Intelligence*, London: Bloomsbury Publishing
Johnson, S (2002) *Who Moved My Cheese?*, New York: GP Putman's Sons
Price, B and Jaffe, D (2008) *The Best Service Is No Service: How to Liberate Your Customers From Customer Service, Keep Them Happy and Control Costs*, San Francisco: Jossey-Bass
Shaw, C and Ivens, J (2002) *Building Great Customer Experiences*, Basingstoke: Palgrave Macmillan
Superbrands(UK) Ltd (2009) *Business Superbrands 2009*, London: Superbrands(UK) Ltd

Taylor, D (2002) *The Naked Leader*, Chichester: Capstone Publishing
van Bennekom, F (2002) *Customer Surveying: A Guide Book For Service Managers*, Bolton, MA: Customer Service Press
Webster, A (2003) *Polar Bear Pirates and their Quest to Reach Fat City*, London: Bantam

Reports/White papers/Journals

Aberdeenshire Customer Service Strategy (2007): http://www.aberdeenshire.gov.uk/about/customerservice/CustomerServiceStrategy.pdf [accessed 18 February 2010]
Accenture (2002/2003) *High-Performance Workforce Study*
Accenture (2007) *Leadership in Customer Service: Delivering on the Promise*
Bazaarvoice and Resource Interactive (2008) *User-Generated Content Research Brief: A look at retailers' perceptions of the importance of user-generated content*
Bright UK Ltd *Bright Performance Management Guide*, 2009
Call centre focus Magazine (2009) 'Budget-busting delays cost call centres dear', September issue.
Court, A (2009) 'Understanding more insight from your customer feedback. Bridge the foreign culture gap – learning to be even more in touch' in *Foreign Culture*, June 2009
Creasy, B (2008) *Effective Focus Groups: A Consultation Institute Best Practice Guide*, Sandy: The Consultation Institute
Cullum, P (2006) *The Stupid Company: How British Businesses Throw Away Money by Alienating Consumers*, National Consumer Council
Customer Care Alliance, The (2008) UK Customer Care Survey: '*Customers: Who Cares?*
Customer Strategy Magazine (2009) 'Player number one has entered the game...' Volume 02 (3), Autumn 2009
Gliedman, C (2008) *The ROI of Interactive Chat*, Independent Forrester Research, Inc., February 4, 2008.
Harvard Business Review (Nov–Dec 1995 and September 2009), *What Service Customers Really Want*
Frost, P, Dutton, C and Ells, H (2007) *Excellence in Managing the Business-to-Business Customer Relationship*, Institute of Customer Service
Institute of Customer Service (2006) *Customer Priorities: What Customers Really Want*

Institute of Directors (2009) *Wellbeing at Work: How to Manage Workplace Wellness to Boost your Staff and Business Performance*

Invomo (2009) *The Invomo Survey: Finding the Perfect Mix*

Johns, T (2008) *World-Class Customer Service: The What, The Why, The How*, Colchester: Institute of Customer Service

Kakkad, A under direction of Voss, C (2006) *Wanted: Chief Experience Officer*, London: London Business School

LaMalfa, K (2007) *The Positive Economics of Customer Engagement*, Allegiance

Marcus, A (2006) *A Demand-Based View of Support: From the Funnel to the Cloud*, San Carlos, CA: Consortium for Service Innovation

Merlin (Undated) 'Knowledge Management: Effective knowledge-enabled self-service solution delivered to clients as a managed service' at: http://www.helpmagic.com/download/Merlin%20Knowledge%20Management%20.pdf

Nokia Siemens Network (2009) *How to Generate Customer Loyalty in Mobile Markets*

Payton, S (2009) 'Attrition 101: how to keep the customers you have' in *Loyalty Management*, Vol 1 (1), a Loyalty 360 publication (www.loyalty360.org)

Oracle (2008) pan-European customer white paper: *Bridging the Divide Between Customer Expectations and Contact Centre Delivery*

Oracle (2009) *Self-service That Really Serves*

People 1st (2008) *Sector Skills Agreement for the Hospitality, Leisure, Travel and Tourism in Scotland* at: http://www.people1st.co.uk/webfiles/Nations/Scotland/Sector_Skills_Agreement_Stage_5_Scotland.pdf [accessed 18 February 2010]

People 1st Sector Skills Council, *World Class Customer Service... for 2012 and Beyond – Summary Report* (2009)

Pine, BJ and Gilmore JH (1998) 'Welcome To The Experience Economy', in *Harvard Business Review*, July–August 1998

Rennstam, M and Jacobs, S (2009) *The Performance Management Guide*, Bright UK Ltd

Strativity Group (2009) *Global Customer Experience Management Benchmark Study*

Thompson, E and Kolsky, E (2004) *How to Approach Customer Experience Management*, Gartner

Unica (2009) Unica White Paper: *Web Analytics to Customer Analytics: Making Web Data Personal* at: http://www.webanalyticsassociation.org/resource_downloads/WP_Unica_Making-Web-Data-Personal_200901.pdf [accessed 18 February 2010]

Valencia, JP under direction of Voss, C (2005) *Experience and the Brand*, London Business School

Van Boven, L and Gilovich, T (2003) 'To Do or to Have? That Is the Question' in *Journal of Personality and Social Psychology*, 85, 1193–1202

Voss, C (2000) *Trusting the Internet: Developing an eService Strategy*, London: Institute of Customer Service

Wall, B (2009) 'The DNA At The Heart Of Your Business: Time to raise the game around customer service delivery' in *Supportworld Magazine*, August/September 2009

West, J (2009) 'Whether forecast?', in *Customer Strategy Magazine*, Volume 02 (3), autumn 2009

BSI publications

Standards

BS 8477:2007 *Code of practice for customer service*
BS EN ISO 9001 *Quality management systems – Requirements*
BS EN ISO 9004:2009 *Managing for the sustained success of an organization – A quality management approach*
BS ISO 10002:2004 *Quality management – Customer satisfaction – Guidelines for complaints handling in organizations*
ISO/TS 10004 *Quality management – Customer satisfaction – Guidelines for monitoring and measuring*
BS ISO 10006:2003 *Quality management systems – Guidelines for quality management in projects*
BS ISO 10007:2003 *Quality management systems – Guidelines for configuration management*
BS 10012 *Data protection – Specification for a personal information management system*
BS ISO/IEC 20000-2:2005 *Information technology – Service management – Code of practice*

Books

BIP 0050 *Data Protection Pocket Guide: Essential Facts at Your Fingertips.*

Web Sources

Abbott, R (2009) 'Contact-centre experts respond to the top five customer complaints' at: www.marketingmagazine.co.uk/news/930327/Contact-centre-experts-respond-top-five-customer-complaints/ [accessed 2 November 2009]

Arussy, L (2009) *To Whom are Customers Loyal?, in Marketing Magazine* at: http://www.mycustomer.com/topic/whom-are-customers-loyal [accessed 4 October 2009]

Ayres, C (2009) 'Revenge is best served cold – on YouTube' at: http://www.timesonline.co.uk/tol/comment/columnists/chris_ayres/article6722407.ece [accessed 11 March 2010]

Big Lottery customer service charter (Undated) at: www.biglotteryfund.org.uk/pub_cust_charter.pdf [accessed 18 October 2009] (Arts Council England; Big Lottery Fund; Heritage Lottery Fund; Olympic Lottery Distributor; Sport England; UK Film Council and UK Sport)

Blackburn, L (2009) Customer First UK at: http://www.customerfirst.org/NewsArticle.aspx?newsid=175 [accessed 9 October 2009]

Bode, K (2009) at: http://www.dslreports.com/shownews/Customers-Unhappy-With-Early-Clearwire-Launches-104511 [accessed 11 October 2009]

Cabinet Office (2009): 'Customer Service Excellence Standard' at http://www.cse.cabinetoffice.gov.uk/aboutTheStandardCSE.do

Caterer Research (2009): 'People 1st delivers two new customer service qualifications' at: http://www.caterersearch.com/Articles/2009/07/15/328698/people-1st-delivers-two-new-customer-service-qualifications.html [accessed 20 October 2009]

Charlton, J. (2009) 'Eureka! The benefits of staff suggestion schemes' at: http://www.personneltoday.com/articles/2005/03/04/28231/eureka-the-benefits-of-staff-suggestion-schemes.html [accessed 2 October 2009]

Chiltern District Council's key performance standards case study (2009) at: http://www.chiltern.gov.uk/site/scripts/documents_info.php?documentID=263&pageNumber=5 [accessed 7 October 2009]

The Consultation Institute (2009) 'Tuesday Topics – 149: Donate Your Experience' at http://www.consultationinstitute.org [accessed 17 November 2009]

Customer Contact Association, at: www.cca-global.com/ [accessed 11 March 2010]

Customer Profiling: Methods to Understanding Your Customers, 2007 at: http://www.morebusiness.com/running_your_business/marketing/Understanding-Customers.brc [accessed 21 September 2009]

Department of Business, Enterprise and Regulatory Reform, at: www.berr.gov.uk/ [accessed 11 March 2010]

Google Example (2009) 'How is the working environment within Google?' at: www.google.com/corporate/culture.html [accessed 4 October 2009]

HCL Employee First (2009) at: http://www.employeefirst.in/hclemployeefirst.htm [accessed 5 October 2009]

Institute of Customer Service Service Mark (2009) at: http://www.instituteofcustomerservice.com/ICS%20ServiceMark.aspx

JANET (UK) (2009) 'JANET Service Description: Version 3' at: http://www.ja.net/documents/publications/policy/sla.pdf [accessed 10 October 2009]

Lowenstein, M (2005) and CustomerThink Corp. at: http://www.customerthink.com/article/let_in_sunshine_customers_help_grow_business [accessed 29 September 2009]

Martin, D (2007) http://www.financeweek.co.uk/item/5137 [accessed 28 September 2009]

Mintel (2009) *The Over 50s* at: http://www.marketresearchworld.net/index.php?option=com_content&task=view&id=2182&Itemid=77 [accessed 14 October 2009]

Mystery Shoppers (2004) 'Hill House Hammond Case Study' at: http://www.mystery-shoppers.co.uk/assets/templates/mystery/downloads/hhh_case_study.pdf [accessed 8 October 2009]

New Brand Experience: Branding Fundamentals (2009) at: Lou Williams http://www.newbrandexperience.co.uk/definition-branding.php [accessed 3 October 2009]

The Office for National Statistics (2009), *Life expectancy continues to rise* at: http://www.statistics.gov.uk/cci/nugget.asp?ID=168 [accessed 8 September 2009]

The official site of the Prime Minister's Office, at: www.number10.gov.uk [accessed 11 March 2010]

Office of Fair Trading at: www.oft.gov.uk [accessed 11 March 2010]

Patient Opinion at: http://www.patientopinion.org.uk/ [accessed 11 March 2010]

Prince 2 Definition at: http://www.prince2.com/what-is-prince2.asp [accessed 10 March 2010]

Rackspace (2009) at: http://www.rackspace.co.uk/rackspace-home/fanatical-support, [accessed 5 October 2009]

Bazaarvoice and Resource Interactive (2008), User-Generated Content Research Brief – A look at retailers' perceptions of the importance of user-generated content, at: http://www.scribd.com/doc/3992895/UGC-Research-Brief-eTail [accessed 11 March 2010]

Richer Sounds (2009) at: http://http://www.qype.co.uk/place/413215-Richer-Sounds-London [accessed 30 September 2009]

Service Desk Institute – Service Desk Manager Standards (2009) at: http://www.sdi-e.com [accessed 18 February 2010]

Singapore International Airlines Achievements (2009) at: http://www.singaporeair.com/saa/en_UK/content/company_info/news/achievements.jsp#Header2 [accessed 6 October 2009]

Smith, S (2009) at: http://www.smithcoconsultancy.com/index.php/customer-experience-ideas/top-customer-experience-tips/ [accessed 1 October 2009]

Smith, D and Mindrum, C (2008) 'How to capture the essence of innovation', in *Accenture Outlook Online Journal*: at: http://www.accenture.com/Global/Research_and_Insights/Outlook/By_Issue/Y2008/captureinnovation.htm [accessed 13 October 2009]

Stowell, C (2009) 'Manchester United: Leadership, Teamwork, Success' at: http://www.cmoe.com/blog/manchester-united-leadership-teamwork-success.htm [accessed 18 February 2010]

Sullivan, M and Siefker, R (2009) 'Winning Customers Through Effective Call Center Management at Zappos' at: http://www.customermanagementiq.com/article.cfm?externalID=725&shownewswindow=1&mac=CMLinkedInQ309&SID=LinkedIn&utm_campaign=Linkedin&utm_medium=SMO&utm_source=e-bim&utm_content=Aug24news&utm_term=CustExpProf [accessed 3 September 2009]

Temkin, B. (2009) 'Customer Experience Matters' at: http://experiencematters.wordpress.com/ [accessed 3 October 2009]

UKCSI survey, July 2009, at: http://ukcsi.com/Latestresults.aspx [accessed 16 November 2009] Website image is reproduced by permission of the Institute of Customer Service

Virgin Trains (2007) 'Passenger Charter' at: http://www.virgintrains.co.uk/docs/PASSENGERS_CHARTER_11_NOV_2007.pdf [accessed 29 October 2009]

White, E (2009) People 1st delivers two new customer service qualifications at: http://www.caterersearch.com/Articles/2009/07/15/328698/people-1st-delivers-two-new-customer-service-qualifications.html [accessed 1 October 2009]

The White House, at: www.whitehouse.gov/blog/2009 [accessed 11 March 2010]

Appendix A

Figures

Figure 1. Experiences Create Value – Kakkad, A under direction of Voss, C (2006) *Wanted: Chief Experience Officer*, London: London Business School

Figure 2. Customer Retention Drivers – Nokia Siemens Network (2009) *How to generate customer loyalty in mobile markets*

Figure 3. Strativity Group (2009) *Customer Experience Consumer Study: Consumers Pay for Exceptional Customer Experiences*

Figure 4. Pyramid of Service – Voss, C (2000) *Trusting the Internet: Developing an eService Strategy*, London: Institute of Customer Service – Diagram by Kendall, H (2009)

Figure 5. World Class Customer Service Diagram – Institute of Customer Service (2008) *World-Class Customer Service*

Figure 6. EFQM Excellence Model (2009) – http://ww1.efqm.org/en/Home/aboutEFQM/Ourmodels/TheEFQMExcellenceModel/tabid/170/Default.aspx [accessed 18 February 2010]

Figure 7. Strativity Group 2009 Customer Experience Consumer Study: *Consumers Pay for Exceptional Customer Experiences*

Figure 8. Contrasting views between CEOs and Customers, Accenture (2007)

Figure 9. Caliper: Customer Service Behaviours (2004)

Figure 10. Motability Operations Service Desk, James Davis, Service Desk Manager September (2008)

Figure. 11. The Best Service Is No Service, Price and Jaffe (2008) (Referenced under Books)

Figure 12. The Evolution of Customer Service, 2009, Lacki, T and Spitale, T (2009) 'Sony Online Entertainment realizes an estimated 50 per cent annual investment return on its Customer Service Strategy' in *ROI Review: Maximizing Returns on Customer Service,* RightNow, Vol. 1 (1)

Figure 13. Anchor Trust SDI Award Entry Paper (2008)

Figure 14. Customer relationship management. Drawn and created by Howard Kendall, author

Figure 15. Chat Solves Broad Spectrum of Customer Needs, Gliedman, C (2008) 'The ROI of Interactive Chat', Forrester Research, Inc., February 4, 2008

Figure 16. UKCSI survey, July 2009, at: http://ukcsi.com/Latestresults.aspx [accessed 18 February 2010]

Figure 17. Bright Performance Management Guide 2009

Figure 18. Customer Importance Rating, Nominet Registrant Satisfaction Survey (2007)

Figure 19. Registrant Customer Satisfaction, Nominet Registrant Customer Satisfaction Survey (2007)

Figure 20. Importance of UGC to Business, Bazaarvoice and Resource Interactive (2008), User-Generated Content Research Brief – A look at retailers' perceptions of the importance of user-generated content, at: http://www.scribd.com/doc/3992895/UGC-Research-Brief-eTail

Figure 21. Impact of UGC, Bazaarvoice and Resource Interactive (2008), User-Generated Content Research Brief – A look at retailers' perceptions of the importance of user-generated content, at: http://www.scribd.com/doc/3992895/UGC-Research-Brief-eTail

Figure 22. SDI Service Desk Metrics report 2007.

Figure 23. Mapping life cycle stages and business goals to initiatives that can be driven by personal web analytics, Unica (2009) White paper: Web Analytics to Customer Analytics: Making Web Data Personal, at: http://www.webanalyticsassociation.org/resource_downloads/WP_Unica_Making-Web-Data-Personal_200901.pdf [Accessed 18 February 2010]

Figure 24. SDI Fujitsu 2009 Excellence Awards Entry

Figure 25. Global CEM Benchmark Study, (2009) **Strativity**

Figure 26. Real-time Feedback Analytics (RFA) systems and benefits, CustomerSat (2009) Measuring ROI of Real Time Feedback Analytics, at: http://www.mycustomer.com/files/siftmedia-mycustomer/customersat-002.pdf [Accessed 18 February 2010]